Strong, Brave, Loved

Other Works by Holley Gerth

You're Already Amazing

You're Already Amazing LifeGrowth Guide

You're Already Amazing LifeGrowth DVD

Do You Know You're Already Amazing?

You're Made for a God-Sized Dream

Opening the Door to Your God-Sized Dream

You're Going to Be Okay

What Your Heart Needs for the Hard Days

You're Loved No Matter What

Fiercehearted

Hope Your Heart Needs

Strong Brave Loved

EMPOWERING REMINDERS OF WHO YOU REALLY ARE

Holley Gerth

a division of Baker Publishing Group
Grand Rapids, Michigan

Published by Revell
a division of Baker Publishing Group
PO Box 6287, Grand Rapids, MI 49516-6287
www.revellbooks.com

Printed in the United States of America

ISBN 978-0-8007-2955-4

Library of Congress Cataloging-in-Publication Control Number: 2019002572

19 20 21 22 23 24 25 7 6 5 4 3 2 1

Contents

Contents

A fiercehearted woman . . .

looks life in the face and says, "You can't beat me."
Knows love is risk but reaches out anyway.
Understands kindness takes real courage.
BELIEVES THE IMPOSSIBLE.
Fights like she's unstoppable.
Dares to find beauty in a ragged soul.
Scandalously picks warm over cool.
Tastes life as a brief, salty-sweet miracle.
Skins her knees, has scars that bear witness.
Defends like a warrior and weeps like a girl.
Makes gentle the new strong, small the new big,
ordinary the new extraordinary.
Sees wrinkles on a face as lines in a victory story.
NEVER GIVES IN, NEVER GIVES UP, NEVER LETS GO.
Chases Jesus with a tender, world-changing wildness.
Lives in your neighborhood or not even on your continent.
Looked back at you from the mirror this morning . . .
and has yet to fully see the force her star-scattering,
mountain-moving, water-walking God created her to be.

Introduction

If you ever get a little tired of life's battles, this is for you.

If you wrestle with fear or insecurity, this is for you.

If you ever feel unsure you're going to have victory, this is for you.

It's for me, too, because I can relate to all the above. I also know what it's like to come to a new place of feeling strong, brave, and loved.

By STRONG I don't mean faking it and trying to hide our limp; I mean knowing we are women in a battle, beautiful warriors who cannot be overcome.

By BRAVE I don't mean reckless or forceful; I mean having the courage to face whatever comes our way, to walk in holy confidence and be okay with what's messy or uncertain.

By LOVED I don't mean what we know in our heads; I mean living in the truth of who God is and who he says we are even when the lies we're tempted to believe are hissing in our ears.

We may not have ever met, but I believe with all my heart that you are a woman created by God who has been placed here for such a time as this. Whatever you're going through now, whatever has happened to you in the past, can't change your identity or destiny.

Introduction

You don't have to be defined by your circumstances.

You don't have to be defeated by your struggles.

You don't have to settle for less than God's best in your life.

I know this is true because I've lived it. In a particularly difficult season, I typed out the words of the "Fiercehearted" piece you read at the start of this book on a plane in the dark, sniffling into a too-small napkin and trying not to scare my seatmate. I felt disappointed by life and I thought about giving up. But Jesus met me in that moment, and what poured out of my heart became the beginning of a life-changing revolution in my world and turned into my book *Fiercehearted.*

After *Fiercehearted* released, thousands of women read it, and through their responses it became clear there was so much more to be said. So this devotional builds on the themes of that book and ties them to Scriptures, prayers, and ways to apply truth in our lives. (You don't need to read *Fiercehearted* to benefit from this devotional. Don't wait another minute to start embracing the victory that's rightfully yours.) Some of the content is brand-new and some has been curated from other places, like my blog and freelance work. Every word has been carefully created and chosen to encourage, equip, and empower you to live as an overcomer.

Wherever you are today, whatever you're going through, I pray Jesus will meet you on these pages like he met me on a plane in the dark when it felt like I didn't have any strength or courage left. I pray he'll rescue your heart and renew your hope. I pray he'll bring you to a new place of feeling strong, brave, and loved that's beyond what might even feel possible right now.

We are made for more than "I'm fine."

We are fiercehearted women; this is our time.

ONE

Dangerous Women

My flesh and my heart may fail,
but God is the strength of my heart
and my portion forever.

Psalm 73:26

I sit in a darkened auditorium with my mom on one side of me and my daughter on the other. The three of us have come to hear Priscilla Shirer as part of her Fervent tour. She talks about who we are as women and all God created us to be. She also shares that we have a very real enemy who would love to see our identity stolen and our purpose thwarted. Then she speaks words that are still ringing in my ears and heart: "What a shame it would be for the enemy to believe more about our potential than we do."[1]

She says that while we struggle sometimes to grasp the truth of who we are, the enemy does not. Even on our worst days, he knows we are daughters of God. He knows we are more than conquerors. He knows we can't be defeated. He knows we are women of destiny with a power within us greater than we can even imagine. His only hope is convincing us to not believe the same.

As I look at my mother and daughter, I feel a sudden, fierce protectiveness. *How dare he,* I think. *How dare he lie to them. How dare he try to steal their joy. How dare he try to make them feel like they are not enough.* And I wonder in that moment if God feels the same about me. After all, we are his family, his girls.

Since that's true, perhaps one of the greatest victories we can win for our heavenly Father is to refuse to live in insecurity. Oh, we call it "humility," but I think that may be just another deception of the enemy. True humility—the kind Jesus demonstrated—is fully knowing who we really are and then choosing to love and serve from that place. And holy confidence is an act of war against the enemy of our hearts.

We are beautifully dangerous women when we know deep down we're loved.

We are beautifully dangerous women when we know deep down we're loved. Because then we have the kind of courage that changes the world one heart at a time.

We are significant threats when we understand we have valuable gifts within us. Because then we actually dare to offer them.

We are wild warriors when we realize we are stronger and braver than we've yet to see. Because then we stop cowering and start swinging our swords.

So let's stop beating ourselves up and instead start beating the real opponent. Let's walk in truth and boldness. Let's carry ourselves like the beloved, strong, fiercehearted daughters of a mighty King. The enemy already knows who we really are . . . let's make sure we truly do too.

God, you are the One who created us. You are our strength, the source of our identity, and our hope for the future. You are the One who gives us victory. Help us hold on to the truth about who we are, no matter what we may face. Amen.

• • • • •

Strength comes from remembering who God says we are. Finish this sentence with a reminder your heart needs today. God says I am . . . (for example: loved, forgiven, accepted).

WE ARE WOMEN AND THIS IS A POWERFUL THING. *It is an echo of God's heart and a display of his glory. . . . Let's be women who know we are not eye candy but works of art, not stereotypes but strong forces, not role-players but world shapers.*

—Fiercehearted

TWO

No More

Therefore, since we are surrounded by such a huge crowd of witnesses to the life of faith, let us strip off every weight that slows us down, especially the sin that so easily trips us up. And let us run with endurance the race God has set before us.

Hebrews 12:1 NLT

I'm driving home from lunch with a new friend, replaying the conversation in my mind. Fear makes my breathing shallow, my heartbeat fast. *What if she doesn't like me? What if I came across all wrong?* I often have moments like this when anxiety gets the best of me and I want to retreat from the whole world.

But this time I pray, "Jesus, help me. I don't understand why I act this way. I want to be free." A simple declaration comes to my heart: I am done running away. From now on, I am running toward.

I don't even fully understand what this means, but I put on my tennis shoes when I get home. I walk out the door and onto the trail behind our house. I turn on my favorite music and run like my life depends on it. *No more, no more, no more*, I say with every step.

I think of all I have run away from . . . how fear has chased me and people-pleasing has set my pace, how anxiety has nipped at my heels like a rogue chihuahua, how the lies have worn me out.

I am done.

I will no longer be a woman who's defined by what she's running from.

In the past, the strategy I've usually decided on in moments like these can be summed up in six words: *be good, do more, try harder*. I convince myself that if I'm perfect and hustle enough and make things happen, then somehow it will all turn out okay. But this strategy has been failing me. I think of a recent evening when I went to bed feeling worn and weary. Sometime past midnight, I woke up in the dark and these words came to my heart: "Not by might nor by power, but by my Spirit" (Zech. 4:6). Another translation says it this way, "You will not succeed by your own strength or by your own power. The power will come from my Spirit" (ICB).

I am done running away.
From now on,
I am running toward.

When I looked up the verse the next morning, I noticed it ends this way: "says the Lord of heaven's armies." I'd been worried because I thought the battle was completely up to me. And all the while I had the Lord of heaven's armies willing to fight on my behalf. We are beloved daughters of God. We are more than conquerors. Nothing is too difficult for us because nothing is impossible for the God within us. He will do it.

I speak these truths to my own soul with each step I take on the trail. I also declare this: I am going to run toward grace. I am going to run toward love. I am going to run toward the wild dreams that beckon me in the distance. I am going to run toward boldness and freedom and holy confidence. I am going to run toward Jesus.

I finish, sweaty and spent on the outside, strong and roaring on the inside. I don't know everything this new perspective means, what exactly I have done. But it feels like something dark and destructive challenged me to a race today.

And I won.

God, you are the One who gives us the courage to stop running away and instead run toward all you have for us. Be our strength in every step today. Amen.

· · · · ·

What have you been running away from in your life or heart? Declare right now that you are done running away and instead you will run toward all God has for you.

I FINISHED RUNNING MY ROUTE EVENTUALLY. *Soaked. Mud-spattered. Smelling terrible. None of it mattered. I'd made it home. "I have fought the good fight, I have finished the course, I have kept the faith"* (*2 Tim. 4:7 NASB*).

—Fiercehearted

THREE

Fight with All Your Heart

In all these things we are more than conquerors through him who loved us. For I am convinced that neither death nor life, neither angels nor demons, neither the present nor the future, nor any powers, neither height nor depth, nor anything else in all creation, will be able to separate us from the love of God that is in Christ Jesus our Lord.

Romans 8:37–39

I settle into a comfy chair in a counselor's office and begin to share the lies that sometimes swirl around in my mind. Like a tornado they threaten to destroy everything in their path. My peace. My joy. My belief that I'm loved.

I say to the counselor, "I know these words aren't true. But in the hard moments, they *feel* true. And that's where I'm stuck." Can you relate? If you've ever felt that way, I want you to know you're not the only one. I also want to reassure you it's possible to beat those lies. Yes, it's not only possible but also your right as a daughter of the King.

As I've already mentioned, for years when I heard lies my default response was "try harder." But after months of counseling, conversations with friends, and time with Jesus, I've learned a new way. These days my response is no longer "try harder" but rather "fight back."

The accusations toward our souls aren't proof of our inadequacy; they're proof that we have an adversary.

And the enemy is not ourselves. There's a reason we use the phrase "beating ourselves up." When we think the problem is us, we become harsh toward our own hearts. But our primary battle isn't against any person—including ourselves. And the lies we hear have the same source as the first lie spoken to Eve in the Garden. If you are a woman in this world, you are at war. It is not optional. And while you may not go roaring into battle, at the very least you need to know basic spiritual self-defense.

That's what I lacked. Even after writing books, even after encouraging thousands of women, I didn't know how to defend my own heart. My husband and I recently watched a TV show in which the hero faces a powerful opponent. At one point the hero becomes weary and takes punch after punch. With tears in my eyes, I said over and over, "Fight back. Please fight back."

It's the same feeling I get when I look at my sisters in Christ. It's the same one I get when I think about how I let my own soul be treated. And it makes me want to shout: ENOUGH. It's time to *fight back*. It's time to guard our hearts. It's time to protect our minds. It's time to stop taking the punches and instead take the victory in Jesus's name.

We are overcomers. We are more than conquerors. We are stronger than we know.

Here's the truth about us no matter what we may hear: We are overcomers. We are more than conquerors. We are stronger than we know, braver than we feel, and loved more than we can even imagine.

God, the weapons our enemy uses against us are often accusations. They can feel true even when they are not. Give us the discernment to know when we are coming under fire and to fight back. You are mighty and you are on our side. Amen.

• • • • •

What's a lie you've battled and the truth that can defeat it?

We are tree-swingers

and baby-rockers and mountain-movers. We are girls. We are women. We are daughters of Eve in a fallen world. This means we will never stop being under attack. But it also means we will never—Dear Jesus, may we never—stop fighting back.

—Fiercehearted

FOUR

Gut Honest

There is no condemnation for those who belong to Christ Jesus.

Romans 8:1 NLT

She sits on a black stool that swivels. The kind you might find at a bar. The sort someone could turn dizzy circles on after a few too many drinks. Perhaps she knew a stool like this when the bottle was her closest friend and she drank deep of secrets. But tonight this stool is on a stage and my friend Christy is perched on it, microphone in hand.[1] She is telling us what it means to be found and freed. To let go of shame and fear. To bid guilt goodbye like a bartender announcing last call.

I watch the faces of the women at round tables as Christy talks. There are head nods and tissues pulled from purses, notes scribbled on white pages. Because even though our stories may be different, we all know what it is to be broken. We know what it is to feel alone. This is the secret the enemy of our hearts would like all of us to believe: *you're the only one.*

No one else has ever wrestled with this issue like one would a scaly-backed alligator determined to drag them to the deep.

No one else has not only opened the door when temptation came knocking but also helped unpack the luggage and handed over the keys to the house.

No one else has put on a false self like a rhinestone tiara from the back of the closet and hoped no one would really notice.

But, of course, *you're not the only one*. We're humans and this is the way of us. Trying to impress. Numbing our pain. Tending our secrets like a night garden. We do this because of guilt and shame. Shame is ultimately the belief that we are unlovable. And because of this, love is the only way to break shame.

Christy talks of this. She calls the women in her life who loved her in the middle of the mess and mayhem, the slipups and setbacks, her "shame breakers." They told her God loved her just as much now as before she did anything wrong. They reminded her that her worst moments did not define her. They helped her believe *she was not the only one*.

From there she slowly started speaking the truth about the struggles within her. She told those she felt safest with first. Then the more Jesus healed her, the more she widened the circle of those who knew her story. Until that circle became big enough to encompass this whole room tonight.

Being fiercehearted begins with simply being willing to say, "This is where I've been. This is where I am today. This is where I hope, by the grace of God, to be tomorrow." It means admitting this first to ourselves, then to Jesus, and then with courage and discernment to at least one other being who has a beating, wandering heart like ours.

The fiercehearted risk the small, huge step of being honest. We embrace the awkward. We step off the pedestal. We take a seat on a black stool that swivels or share that we're not fine with a friend over coffee or shout and cry on our knees in front of the God who loves us as we are. We also celebrate unexpectedly and dance like no one's watching and throw the confetti at midnight. We embrace all the parts of our unexpected, mysterious, still-being-written story.

Strong, brave, and loved sometimes looks like just the opposite. And that's beautiful.

We do this because we understand that strong, brave, and loved sometimes looks like just the opposite.

And that's beautiful.

God, you know everything about us and you love us anyway. Give us the courage to embrace our story, even the parts we wish were different. Amen.

• • • • •

Pause for a few moments and tell God how you really are today—struggling, happy, sad, disappointed, tired, angry, frustrated, afraid. If shame or guilt try to creep in, say Romans 8:1 out loud.

I WANT ALL OF US TO FEEL LESS ALONE *and more comfortable in our God-sewn skin and a little surer we are a force to be reckoned with in this world.*

—Fiercehearted

FIVE

Joy Guarding

Our struggle is not against flesh and blood, but against the rulers, against the authorities, against the powers of this dark world and against the spiritual forces of evil in the heavenly realms. Therefore put on the full armor of God, so that when the day of evil comes, you may be able to stand your ground, and after you have done everything, to stand.

Ephesians 6:12–13

Some days the thoughts still come like an assault as soon as I open my eyes . . .

You're not doing enough.

You're letting people down.

When are you going to get it together?

A few years ago, I uttered a frustrated prayer in my car. "God, why does the enemy seem so determined to destroy my joy?" And it felt like I heard a whisper within my heart in response: "He's not really after your joy. He's after your strength."

Immediately I thought of Nehemiah 8:10: "The joy of the Lord is your strength." Ah, yes, now it made sense.

The enemy of my soul wasn't simply out to make me have a bad day. Instead, he was trying to do something far more sinister: Make me ineffective in the kingdom. Weaken my faith. Quiet my voice. Make sure I cower in fear rather than stand in faith.

We've all probably had well-meaning people say to us, "Just be joyful!" like it's an easy thing. As if the moment we decided to follow Jesus our lives would be cotton-candy happy forever, so we should just get with the program. But here's the truth: Joy requires all-out war. Every day. For the rest of our lives.

Here's the good news: We aren't fighting alone. God is with us, for us, and on our side. He is even more committed to our victory than we are. As we just talked about, "In all these things we are more than conquerors through him who loved us" (Rom. 8:37). We just have to be willing to join the battle.

We're told to put on the armor of God, and there is only one offensive weapon in it: "The sword of the Spirit, which is the word of God" (Eph. 6:17). We guard our joy with truth. When the lies come, we have to slash them with what God says instead.

God is with us, for us, and on our side. He is even more committed to our victory than we are.

You're not doing enough. Truth: I only have to do what Jesus wants me to today, and he will enable me to do so. "I can do all this through him who gives me strength" (Phil. 4:13).

You're letting people down. Truth: I'm not perfect, so sometimes I will let people down. What matters is being obedient to God. "If pleasing people were my goal, I would not be Christ's servant" (Gal. 1:10 NLT).

When are you going to get it together? Truth: I'm human, and as long as I'm on earth, I'll still be in progress. But God is growing me each day. "He who began a good work in you will carry it on to completion until the day of Christ Jesus" (Phil. 1:6).

We don't have to believe the enemy. We're not weaklings. We're warriors. So let's stand firm. Raise the sword of truth. Never surrender our joy. It's time to fight like women who belong to the God who can never be defeated—which means we can't be either.

God, may your love always be louder than the lies. We will live in the truth. We will guard our joy. We will listen to your voice. You give us the strength to fight and to win. Amen.

• • • • •

How has the enemy tried to take your joy?
What's one way you can guard it today?

We are worth fighting for too.

God loves all his kids alike. It's only us who differentiate. Who tell ourselves that everyone and everything else is deserving of our courage and compassion and fierceness but us. This is one of the trickiest lies. Please don't believe it.

—*Fiercehearted*

SIX

Defend Your Sisters

Therefore encourage one another and build each other up, just as in fact you are doing.

1 Thessalonians 5:11

Women tell me how words have wounded them. They walk into my counseling office and bare the scars on their hearts. They lean into me at blogging conferences and whisper of unkind comments. They confide in me over coffee—the hurt echoing all the way back from childhood. I nod my head because I understand. I've been there too. "The words of the reckless pierce like swords" (Prov. 12:18).

Yes, words can be weapons.

It takes only a careless remark. A bit of gossip. A little less sensitivity in a stress-filled moment. *Do we know what we do to our sisters?*

I sit alone and pray about this one day. I've become afraid of words—of what they can do. And it seems in the dark I sense a whisper. "Daughter, words can defend and protect too." It's right there in our armor like we've talked about already: "The sword of the Spirit, which is the word of God" (Eph. 6:17).

We must choose how we wield our words.

In my heart, I once pictured the enemy coming and a wounded woman on the ground behind me. I put my sword in front of her and said, "You can't have her. She belongs to the King." I still get goose bumps as I put those words on this page, because *this is why I write*. Because life is hard and we all fall and we need sisters who stand in the gap for us. Because words have the capacity to hold back evil, to bring forth life, to sustain, encourage, and unite us.

Words are powerful.

And if we think ours aren't part of a battle much bigger than us, it's time to think again.

So what do we do with this knowing, this sword that's in our hands? Sisters, let's put our words firmly on the side of the kingdom and use them to protect, never to harm. I'm raising my sword and pledging my allegiance to you and to the One Who Loves Us. Will you join me?

A Commitment of Words

We commit to using our WORDS to defend and heal, not to harm.

We will not gossip.

We will not belittle.

We will guard our sisters by always SPEAKING the best about them, encouraging them into all God would have them to be, and offering grace instead of condemnation.

We will be loyal and loving, remembering that even if we disagree, we still fight on the same side—never against each other.

We will use our WORDS to build up and not tear down, to bring hope and not hurt.

We offer our WORDS as powerful weapons to fight for each other on the side of all that is good, right, and true.

Defend Your Sisters

Women tell me how words have healed them. They walk into my counseling office and share the encouragement planted in their hearts. They lean into me at blogging conferences and whisper of grace-giving comments. They confide in me over coffee—the hope echoing all the way back from childhood. Do we know what we do *for* our sisters?

So let's choose to wield our words in ways that change the world . . . starting with each other.

Words matter and make a difference.

The choice of how we will use them is ours to make. So let's choose to wield our words in ways that change the world . . . starting with each other.

God, we want our words to be weapons for your kingdom. Help us protect, defend, and encourage our sisters with what we say. We will fight for those around us. Amen.

. . . . .

When has someone spoken encouraging words to you? What did they say and how did it make a difference?

FRIENDSHIP IS REALLY ALL ABOUT HELPING *each other become who God intends for us to be tomorrow.*

—Fiercehearted

SEVEN

Worshiper and Warrior

Be strong and take heart,
all you who hope in the Lord.

Psalm 31:24

Our God. . . . We do not know what to do . . ." (2 Chron. 20:12). Haven't we all been in that place? The one where the answers don't come. The plans are uncertain. Where everyone is counting on us and we want to count the steps to the exit.

What will we put after the second pause in that sentence? Here are a few ways I've completed it.

"I do not know what to do . . . so I'm going to eat another brownie."

"I do not know what to do . . . so I'm going to listen to the latest expert."

"I do not know what to do . . . so I'm going to try harder to please everyone."

We all have our favorites. And we can all probably learn from Jehoshaphat, who first spoke those words when a vast army was approaching. Because in that hard, scary moment, he said this: "Our God, we do not know what to do, but our eyes are on you."

When we face challenging circumstances, we think we must know what to do, but in reality, all we really need to know is Who is on our side. Because that's what makes the difference. That's what matters on the hard days. That's what brings the victory.

After this declaration, Jehoshaphat did something we won't find in any war instruction book or military briefing. He put the worshipers in front of the army. He led not with the generals but with the singers and the praisers, the choir members.

Truth is a powerful weapon. And the truest thing of all is who God is. His character is a fortress and battering ram, an all-out assault against evil. This means worship is absolutely undefeatable.

Perhaps, too, the worshipers needed to go first as an act of war against fear. This battle didn't look easily won. The Israelites were outnumbered, weary, and seemingly ready to be overrun.

Haven't we felt like that sometimes too? And in those moments, isn't fear really our biggest enemy? It's our Goliath, challenging us, and we are the trembling soldiers trying to put on our man-made armor. Because we know what is human is not going to be enough. Then we realize we have another option. Praise is the sling and the stones. The secret weapon. Stronger than our solutions. Mightier than our education and experience. More effective than a thousand bullet points.

So if we are unsure about what to do today, if the enemy is coming and the battle is raging and maybe we have even been wounded—let us stand our ground and raise our voices. Let us speak the truth about who God is and what he has done. How big he is. How much he loves us. How he has always held the universe and our little part of it in his hands.

We cannot lose with him. We cannot be overcome.

We cannot be overcome.

As I stood listening to the music of praise in a crowded room recently, I saw a few of my sisters with their arms raised. I know their stories. I've seen their scars. I realized those hands lifted to heaven weren't empty—they were holding invisible swords. Not for fighting each other but for battling an unseen enemy.

Jehoshaphat won his battle. We will too.

To be a worshiper is to be a warrior.

God, we praise you because you are powerful, wise, and kind. You love us more than we could ever imagine. You are our strength, our hope, and the One who makes us fiercehearted women. Amen.

• • • • •

Praise is powerful. Take a moment to praise God—write it down, say it out loud, or even sing it.

We are mightier than we know,

more courageous than we feel, and we belong to a God who has promised all this is temporary. Someday the war will be over, the tears will be wiped away, and we will be strong forever.

—Fiercehearted

EIGHT

Make Friends with Fear

So do not fear, for I am with you;
do not be dismayed, for I am your God.
I will strengthen you and help you;
I will uphold you with my righteous right hand.

Isaiah 41:10

I sit in the front row and quietly shake in my cute red boots. They're supposed to make me feel a bit more like a superhero, but they're not working so well tonight. I laugh to myself at the irony. In a few minutes, I'll step onto the stage and speak at a conference about anxiety. Yet as I wait, my heart races and I inwardly pray for calm.

One of my fellow speakers confesses that it has always seemed like a paradox for God to tell us, "Do not be afraid," and yet give us bodies that are wired to experience fear. As a licensed counselor and certified life coach, I've studied a lot about how our brains work. We actually can't help it when our nervous system triggers our fight-or-flight response. It's automatic and always involves fear. So if we're "wonderfully made" like the psalmist says, then how do we reconcile what God seems to tell us to *do* with how he's created us to *feel*?

As someone who has wrestled with fear for most of my life, I've asked that question often. And as I looked closer at what God says, I finally found my answer. Verses that say "Do not be afraid" are almost always spoken to or for someone who is *already* afraid.

Israelite armies about to go into battle (see Deut. 20:1–4).

Mary being startled by an unexpected angel (see Luke 1:30).

The apostle Paul facing a serious storm (see Acts 27:23–26).

In other words, when God says, "Do not be afraid," it is most often offered as a reassurance, not issued as a command. He's not saying, "Don't ever feel fear." He's saying, "Here's why you don't have to *stay* afraid."

> *Do not fear, for I am with you.* (Isa. 41:10)

> *Do not fear;*
> *I will help you.* (Isa. 41:13)

> *Do not fear . . .*
> *I have called you by your name; you are mine.* (Isa. 43:1 CSB)

It's the kind of language a loving parent would use to comfort a child who's afraid of the dark. A compassionate mom or dad knows their little one is going to be okay, but they give words that soothe hearts and calm minds anyway. And most beautiful of all, their love defeats the fear.

If we wait to do God's will until we don't ever feel fear, then we will stay stuck. He's okay with our trembling hands, knocking knees, and pounding hearts. After all, he designed our human bodies—and he spent thirty-three years in one. When we experience anxiety or fear, the enemy can try to use it as an opportunity to make us feel guilt or shame. That's when we can pause and ask God for help, knowing he understands and never condemns us.

God will come alongside us in our uncertain moments and give us the reassurance we need.

God will come alongside us in our uncertain moments and give us the reassurance we need. Then he'll lead us out of fear and into courage. Cute red boots aren't even required. (Although in my professional opinion, they're still highly recommended.)

God, you created every part of us, including our emotions. Thank you that our fear is not a surprise to you. You are always willing to encourage us and help us be brave. Amen.

• • • • •

What's a truth that helps you be brave? For example, "God is always with me" or "I can do all this through him who gives me strength" (Phil. 4:13).

We're all a bit afraid.

We all want to belong. We all worry we will be too much or not enough. So let's be brave today. Let's love and be loved. Let's look with gentler eyes at ourselves and each other.

—*Fiercehearted*

NINE

Show Up Anyway

Be on your guard; stand firm in the faith; be courageous; be strong.

1 Corinthians 16:13

I drift tentatively through the door of a ministry event along with other women. We scan the room and look for seats. *A place to belong.* Isn't that what everyone wants? Each spot at every table has a little plate with a miniature dessert on it. Sugary shapes set out like welcome mats. I choose a chocolate cupcake.

We talk and laugh, a speaker shares, and then it's time for discussion questions. The first one: *What makes you feel brave?*

The women at my table have inspiring answers. One talks about worship music and how the words move her soul. Another speaks of friends who encourage. A woman with a bright smile says simply obeying is what does it in her life. I can barely come up with an answer. I consider copying someone else's. Instead, I say something about thinking back on what God has already done in my life. I also give another shout-out to my red cowboy boots, the same ones I wear whenever my knees start knocking and I need to tap into my inner Wonder Woman.

But all my replies feel uncertain to me, as if I've left out something important and true. Alone in my room later that evening, I realize it's this: *I never feel brave.* When this thought first pops into my mind, I try to deny it. Surely I do sometimes. Yet I can't think of a single time brave showed up as an emotion in my world.

I know what it is to *be* brave. But in those times, what I feel first is still fear. The pounding of my heart and quickening of my breath. The spinning of the earth beneath my feet and sense that I may be full-out crazy to go through with what I'm about to do. As I think about this, I realize maybe I've misunderstood what brave feels like. I thought it was a roar and a lunge. But maybe it is a whisper and a trembling step. I thought it was loud and bold. Perhaps it is quiet and almost invisible. I thought it meant the absence of all insecurity. Yet I'm wondering now if bravery is just faith dancing the two-step with doubt.

If this is so, then what makes me act brave is also what scares me silly.

Bravery is just faith dancing the two-step with doubt.

This lets me breathe a sigh of relief because it means I don't have to wait to be filled with confidence before I can do anything. I can just show up anyway. If that's so, then I have more courage than I thought. And more answers than I realize, including the one I wish I'd had at the round table with those lovely folks. If I could go back to that moment, I'd say, "I'm not sure what makes me brave, but I know *Who* does. And I know what being brave makes us—strong, fierce, and a force to be reckoned with in this world."

God, you give us so much more than just emotion; you give us your presence, power, truth, and help. Even when we're afraid, we can show up and be brave because we belong to you. Amen.

What's a time when you felt afraid and did something hard or scary anyway? How did God help you?

HERE'S TO WHATEVER BRINGS US TO THE POINT *where we can no longer stay the same. Here's to keeping the front door open. Here's to doing the brave, hard thing.*

—Fiercehearted

TEN

Not Ready

My grace is sufficient for you, for my power is made perfect in weakness.

2 Corinthians 12:9

I'm an amateur eavesdropper. I often work in coffee shops, where conversations swirl around me as thick as the scent of espresso. Most of the time I'm able to tune them out, but sometimes one makes my head snap up from my laptop. I've heard scandalous confessions of love, details of doctor's appointments, and workplace complaints of all sorts. This morning I found myself the recipient of some unsolicited wisdom.

A young man and his mentor sat next to me talking about faith. Apparently they've been meeting for a while, because the young man asked, "When am I going to be ready to help someone else?"

The mentor paused and then answered, "I think you're asking the wrong question. Because as long as you ask, 'Am I ready?' you'll always be able to find a reason you're not. A flaw. A struggle. Something you think you need to learn more about. The better question to ask is, 'Have I received something?' If so, then you have something to share. When is the best time to start passing it on? Yesterday."

I looked over for a second just to be sure he wasn't talking to me. Because I have wondered this as well. Haven't we all? Here is a secret of faith I'm learning: We never feel qualified. We never feel like professionals. We never feel like we've got it together enough to really make a difference. And maybe this is a good thing. Because the only folks who seem to have believed otherwise were the Pharisees.

God is not looking for perfect examples. He's looking for ordinary people who will love each other. He's calling the messy, the broken, and the incomplete. This is good news for all of us. It means Jesus will give to us and then he'll give through us. We're simply asked to be willing and brave enough to do it as we are and not as we'd like to be.

God is not looking fo perfect examples. He's looking for ordin people who will love each other.

My heart needed to hear all of this today. Maybe yours did too. Perhaps sometime we'll run into each other at a coffee shop and can talk it over. And when we're done, I'll try very hard not to eavesdrop on you.

God, you show your power in the most unexpected ways and people. Where we see weaknesses, you see opportunities. Thank you that we don't have to be perfect to be used by you; we only need to be willing. Amen.

• • • • •

What's one small way you can bless, help, or encourage someone today—even if you don't feel fully confident or totally ready?

THERE IS A TIME FOR BEING STILL, *for waiting. But if we know that this is not what we are doing, that we are simply delaying because we're scared or feeling a bit inadequate, then it's time to go anyway. . . . None of us are ready. All of us are afraid.*

—Fiercehearted

ELEVEN

Messy Again

Though your sins are like scarlet,
they shall be as white as snow;
though they are red as crimson,
they shall be like wool.

Isaiah 1:18

I take my seat and eye the blank canvas in front of me with suspicion. I'm here for a guided painting party, and we all laugh nervously as we consider the task before us. Then someone says, "The good news is you can paint over any canvas."

Those words keep repeating in my mind and echoing in my heart—"You can paint over any canvas." They make me recall the reassurance offered in 1 Peter 4:8: "Love covers over a multitude of sins." In other words, love can paint over any canvas.

Yes, even that choice we made that feels like it could never be forgiven.

Yes, the secret that sometimes wakes us up in the middle of the night.

Yes, those mistakes that accuse us from the quiet, dark corners of our hearts.

The enemy would like to tell us, "You don't get a second chance." But the scandalously gracious Savior we serve says, "I died to give you as many chances as you need."

If we believe that we can never mess up, we'll be paralyzed with fear. We'll sit like I did and stare at the blank canvas of our lives without ever even taking hold of the brush God wants to place in our hands. Yes, we'll keep it all nice, neat, and clean. But there will be no beauty. There will be no boldness. There will be no inexplicable glory among the mess.

We live in urgent times. And this world doesn't need safe saints; it needs fiercehearted followers who know they will not get it right but are willing to try anyway. It needs courage and color and the smudge of a heart spilled out.

I finally place the first stroke on the canvas. Then another. And another. With the instructor's voice as my guide, a vision gradually begins to become reality. By the end, I lean back and smile. Is my painting perfect? No. Does it look exactly like the example? No. But does it bring me joy anyway? Yes. And to my surprise, I no longer want to cover up what I've done. Because somehow the places where I messed up add to the story, to the humanity, to the sense I have been part of a becoming.

Art isn't about perfection. It's about being brave enough to try. Life is too.

I learn a few painting tricks and tips. But what I learn even more is this: Art isn't about perfection. It's about being brave enough to try. Life is too. Every day is a blank canvas. So let's grab our brushes, pick our colors, and begin . . . again.

God, thank you for forgiving us over and over again. Thank you for what you did on the cross to pay for all our sin. We receive your gift, your extraordinary love, and your mercy. We will walk in freedom and grace. Amen.

• • • • •

Was there a sin or struggle that came to mind as you read this piece? If so, pause to let grace and forgiveness take the place of any shame and guilt. I am forever forgiven for . . .

Let's make this our declaration:

instead of trying to have it all together, we will dare to do real, messy, imperfect life all together.

—Fiercehearted

TWELVE

Love over Fear

There is no fear in love. But perfect love drives out fear, because fear has to do with punishment. The one who fears is not made perfect in love. We love because he first loved us.

1 John 4:18–19

Loving other people can feel like stepping across a field of land mines sometimes. Perhaps this is truest of all online. Politics. Social issues. The latest offense at school or work or the fast-food drive-through. They're all there. Angry words, sharp-pointed opinions, the shrapnel of bitterness and envy. Why do we do this to each other?

I've come to believe this: *we are most angry when we are most afraid.* It's the old fight-or-flight response built into our bodies from the beginning. Some of us flee, but others of us pick up our guns and load them with words. We think we are saving ourselves, maybe even saving the world, but we are destroyers in disguise.

I recently talked about this with two friends and fellow writers. During our conversation, this verse came to mind: "There is no fear in love. But perfect love drives out fear" (1 John 4:18). We, as humans, tend to think if we can have things our way, then the world will be better. So we fight our fear aggressively and forcefully. We post and shout. We raise our fists and our voices.

But what if instead of spewing those angry words and that tirade online, we simply go to the person who is standing in our kitchen today and say, "I love you and I am for you"? Or we reach out to someone who is different from us? Because we also fear what we don't understand. And if we're spending all our time saying, "Here's my opinion," then we're not listening, not understanding. Fear wins.

One of my friends asked, "What would it be like if we made a commitment to fight *for* each other instead of *with* each other?"[1] It's a question worth considering if we want to defeat fear. Because if we live with swords drawn in defense, then we are always on guard, looking for the next fight, seeing threatening shadows in every corner.

We have a Protector. He is good. He is wise. He is kind. And here's what we need to know: *God hasn't asked us to be right all the time. He has called us to love*. This is the harder, braver choice. Because it requires opening our hearts instead of our mouths. It's about seeing each other not as threats but as people made in the image of God. It means we lay down our weapons and go, with arms wide open, down a path that could very well lead to a cross.

Love is stronger than fear.

At first we might be scared. This is not the easy option, after all. But it is the fiercehearted one. And it's the only way back to grace and peace, mercy and hope, humility and kindness.

I still believe this: love is stronger than fear.

God, you are the maker of all human beings, those we care for most and the ones who will always be a mystery to us. Give us eyes to see others as you do, hearts that have compassion like yours, and the strength to keep on loving. Amen.

. . . . .

Think of one person who is sometimes hard for you to love and take a moment to pray for them. God, you know it's challenging for me to love this person sometimes, and today I ask you to . . .

WHILE THE DETAILS ARE DIFFERENT, *in so many ways our stories are the same. They are all full of anger and fear, struggle and loss, hope and longing.*

—Fiercehearted

THIRTEEN

Strong, Soft

Therefore everyone who hears these words of mine and puts them into practice is like a wise man who built his house on the rock. The rain came down, the streams rose, and the winds blew and beat against that house; yet it did not fall, because it had its foundation on the rock.

Matthew 7:24–25

The wind blows cold against my back as I walk along the streets in the quiet suburb where I live. I think of other days when I've walked this same path with much on my mind. Losses. Hurts. Dreams laid down.

And I think of loved ones who have felt the chilly breath of trouble on their hopes too. Mamas who have said goodbye to babies. Teens who have survived abuse. Folks who have battled cancer. It's a cold world sometimes. Some of those folks have come out of those times with greater strength, tenderness, and resilience. Others have become bitter and hard. I quietly ask myself, "What makes the difference?"

As I ponder this question, I think back to one particularly painful season in my life. It seemed sorrow, frustration, and disappointment threatened to overtake me. I wanted to shut down my heart, lock the door of my life, and let bitterness move in as my only companion. Yet God seemed to keep whispering, “Yield, yield, yield.”

I grew up in a place where hurricanes were frequent, and I learned this: the trees that survive are the ones that bend. Tough times do one of two things—they reshape us or they break us. And the choice is up to us.

If we stiffen our souls and harden our hearts, then the wind blows against us until we break to our core. But if we can bend—keep trusting, hoping, loving—then we are transformed in ways beyond our understanding.

Oh, we will have days when we experience deep grief and anger. That’s okay—it’s actually part of yielding. We let ourselves feel our emotions and wave them wildly for a bit like branches. It’s when we stop feeling that we should begin to worry. When we fake it. Or when we insist on having our own way. When we quit believing God is good because he did not give us what we wanted.

I’ve talked with thousands of women about life’s difficulties. And I have found this: It is not the circumstances or even the depth of the hurt that determines who heals. It’s the response. Those who somehow thrive never lose their softness. You can see it in their eyes. You can hear it in their voices. You can tell it by the way they are still kind to others. Oh, they are fierce, these women. Tenderness and tenacity are sisters. But they are not steel inside. Yes, here’s the secret we can cling to when the wind comes: life is hard, but our hearts do not have to be . . . because of Jesus.

Life is hard, but our hearts do not have to be . . . because of Jesus.

When he is our security, we don’t have to protect ourselves by stiffening our souls. We don’t have to make ourselves “unbreakable” because we are so afraid. We don’t have to shut out anything that might make us weak—like love, hope, or kindness. We can be brave.

As I reach my house again, the wind has stilled to almost a whisper. The trees are at peace. They stretch their branches high toward the last of the sun's rays. It looks like an act of hope. Or perhaps of praise.

God, you understand how hard it is to live in this world sometimes. You know how to handle hurt and fear while still choosing love and grace. Help our hearts be both strong and tender like yours. Amen.

• • • • •

Who in your life has gone through tragedy or difficulty and still kept a soft heart? What have you learned from them?

Having a soft heart

in a hard world is courage, not weakness.

—Fiercehearted

FOURTEEN

Better Than You Know

One thing I do: Forgetting what is behind and straining toward what is ahead, I press on toward the goal to win the prize for which God has called me heavenward in Christ Jesus.

Philippians 3:13–14

I am an awkward runner—not gracefully athletic but more like an enthusiastic, uncoordinated giraffe. I have learned to accept this. I go anyway.

I feel the pavement beneath my feet with every step. The hill taunts me and tries to steal my breath. But what really makes me want to quit are the accusations inside: *You're going so slow. You're not doing a good job. This must be your worst run ever.*

I used to listen to that voice, until I discovered something: every time I heard it, I ended up with a time that was my personal best.

Because the reality is, in the moments when we want to give up, when we feel weak and exhausted, when we think we can't do it . . . we're actually getting stronger.

We're not tired because we're failing; we're tired because we're fighting.

We're not weary because we're weak; we're weary because we're winning the battle to go to the next level in our lives.

This is the scandalous secret: when we want to quit, it really means we're making progress.

So I'm learning to hear that voice in a different way. When those accusations come (which they still do), I think, *I must be running harder and faster than ever before—it just doesn't feel like it*. It's often the same in the rest of our lives too.

Let's not allow the enemy of our hearts to convince us to stop because we think we're not doing well enough. Instead, let's recognize the effort and the pain for what they are—signs of growth.

Yes, sometimes the hurt means we are injured and need to rest. But often it simply means we are breaking through what has held us back and pushing with all our might toward what God has for us.

In the place between what is comfortable and what seems like it will surely kill us is often where we become all we're created to be.

In the place between what is comfortable and what seems like it will surely kill us is often where we become all we're created to be.

I finish my run and, sure enough, I've dropped almost a minute from my time. It seems small, but to me it's huge. I'm not taking that victory lightly. I've earned every teeth-gritting second of it. I didn't quit. And I didn't die. In this world, that's the best and bravest we can do some days.

The voices inside are finally silent, so it's my turn to speak. I say to all the lies that chased me and nipped at my heels, "I'm stronger than you think."

Even if I don't always feel it, I'm learning to believe it.

God, you are the One who keeps us going. You are the One who gives us strength and courage for the next step. You are the One who will see us through all the way to the finish line. Amen.

• • • • •

What's one small step of faith, love, or courage you can take today? Today I will . . .

NEVER GIVE ANYONE OR ANYTHING *the power to shame you. You're braver than you feel, stronger than you know, and loved more than you've yet to see.*

—Fiercehearted

FIFTEEN

Live True

Jesus said, "If you hold to my teaching, you are really my disciples. Then you will know the truth, and the truth will set you free."

John 8:31–32

The early morning sun is just slanting through the windows when I roll over and reach for the switch on the lamp. I am not a morning person and my eyes beg to close again. Instead, I grab a small white note card and thick black pen. This has become my habit. Each day I seek out a name of God in Scripture and write it down. I also record truth in a plain spiral-bound notebook, the flimsy kind kids carry to school in backpacks.

I do this because my heart is forgetful. I could have known the day before who God is and who I am, but night comes and it slips away. I wake to a new day, and unless I'm very intentional, I can live in a fog of doubt and fear, insecurity and uncertainty. I have come to understand God says his mercies are new every morning because that's how often we need them.

I have also come to understand this: being "loved" means living daily out of the truth of who God is and who he says we are. This is what empowers us to be strong, what gives us the guts to be brave. It is the fortress our hearts can go back to when war and chaos are all around us.

The stack of cards by my bed has grown. It tells me that God is love. It reminds me that he is my defender. It whispers to me that he is the purpose-giver and peace-bringer and Creator of all. No matter what this day holds, none of this will change. He is forever the same.

In my journal, I record what I'm grateful for and who I am, based on this reality. Because God is love, I am loved. Because God is my defender, I can't be defeated. Because God is my purpose-giver, I have an identity and destiny. Because he is my peace-bringer, I can walk in rest and trust. Because he is my Creator, I can be confident in who he has made me.

True confession: Sometimes all of this is hard to believe. Sometimes I don't feel it; my emotions can take a long time to catch up with what's true. Sometimes I fall back asleep and drool on my pillow. I've learned all of this is okay. What matters most is that I keep coming back to the One who came for me.

The great big world will tell us that what we need to thrive is somewhere "out there." It's in relationships or money or the next vacation. Maybe it's hidden in the closet of the big house or in the sole of the high-heeled shoe. But I've discovered in the quiet of early morning that what we need, what we crave most, is right at our fingertips and in our hearts. What we really long for in all our longings is God himself.

Eventually I sit up and my feet touch the stretched and stained carpet. I don't know what this day will bring, but I know what will not change. I am God's daughter. I am beloved. I have everything I need for whatever I may face. Today I can walk in the truth of who I am and Whose I am.

I am God's daughter. I am beloved. I have everything I need for whatever I may face.

God, we're so grateful that who you are never changes. And you are the One who ultimately tells us who we are. Help us stay true to you and who you've created us to be today. Amen.

• • • • •

What's a name of God that really resonates with your heart? Write it on a little piece of paper and carry it with you today. God is . . .

[GOD] OFFERS WHAT SHE LONGS FOR MOST—*for him to tell her who she really is, to whisper in her ear that he has made her funny and wise and strong and brave. That she is tender and resilient and complex and wonder-filled. She is mystery and unveiling. She is salty tears and the sweat at the finish line and the lioness in the corner office and lullabies in the night.*

—Fiercehearted

SIXTEEN

As Is

Accept one another, then, just as Christ accepted you, in order to bring praise to God.

Romans 15:7

I take a deep breath and step out of my car. I'm getting together with two friends. One I've known for years. She's already aware of my faults and quirks. She's seen my hair at its best and worst. We've shed tears and shared laughter. I'm safe with her. But the other girl joining us is someone I don't know as well yet. I like her—she's smart, funny, and creative. I really want her to think the same of me.

With the second friend, I notice I'm more aware of what I say and how I respond to questions. I try a little harder to be funny or maybe even a bit cool (which never works for me). I analyze the conversation instead of just letting my words flow freely. At some point I realize what I'm doing and pause for a moment. *What is this all about?*

I've bought into the lie that if I can just make this new girl think I'm perfect, then surely we'll be friends. But I look at my other friend, the one who's been in my life forever, and know right then this isn't going to be an effective tactic.

Because what we really want aren't people we can impress; we want people who will love us *anyway.*

The reality is, I'm a flawed human being. I'm not perfect today, and I won't be tomorrow, next year, or on the day I take my final breath. I'm also a woman created by God with strengths, gifts, and much to offer. We all are.

We need to be true to who we are, to show up as is, because that's the only way we actually feel less alone.

What we really need from each other is not a pared-down version of ourselves that's been polished and carefully presented. We need to be true to who we are, to show up as is, because that's the only way we actually feel less alone.

I decide then and there to stop trying so hard. I let my shoulders relax and lean into the conversation so I can be fully present instead of lost in my own worries. Maybe this friendship will grow—I hope so. But if not, that will be okay too. We don't need the whole world to love us as we are (that's impossible); we just need a few brave folks. And the best way to start finding those grace-givers is to dare to be one of them ourselves.

God, you've placed us in community with others not to prove we're perfect but to be loved as we are and to grow into all you want us to be. Help us to be honest about our struggles as well as our strengths, to share our hurts and victories. Give us the grace and courage to love others as they are too. Amen.

• • • • •

When do you feel tempted to hold back who you are or try to be someone you're not? What helps you dare to be who you really are in those situations?

We are shifting kaleidoscopes

of strangeness and brilliance, weakness and strength, courage and fear, glory and falling, one-of-a-kind and a-lot-like-everyone-else.

—*Fiercehearted*

SEVENTEEN

Love Long and Real

Speaking the truth in love, we will grow to become in every respect the mature body of him who is the head, that is, Christ. From him the whole body, joined and held together by every supporting ligament, grows and builds itself up in love, as each part does its work.

Ephesians 4:15–16

I walk along the creek bed, with summer grass brushing the edges of my feet. I try to block the sun from my eyes with my hand as I stare at the line of trees. I'm looking for a place I haven't visited since childhood—a long rope dangling from a limb my friends and I dubbed "the swing" that I write about in *Fiercehearted*. We spent adventurous hours here and came home covered in sweat and dust, only to add a layer of sticky Popsicle juice.

As I continue my search, I think more about the relationships I had then and the childlike faith with which we whooped and hollered, dared and played, ran wild and roamed free. What I can forget as a grown-up is how essential the willingness to be a little crazy is to this type of living. We never worried too much about mud or dirty knees or spilled sodas. It was all part of the ruckus and fun. Our goal wasn't to come home clean; it was to come home spent and wonder-filled.

I want to go back to that kind of carefree wisdom when I am with the people I trust. To drop my guard and lay it all out. To laugh so hard the salsa falls right off my chip and onto the restaurant table with a splat. To let the tears flow until the mascara streaks run down my cheeks like a little winding river. To walk back through the door of my house feeling bolder and stronger than before.

We need to be human together—to share the hard and the happy, the struggles and the victories. Because in doing so, we remember and remind each other that we are not God. This is the beginning of worship. And we need to understand that we're loved as we are. This is the beginning of joy.

> We need to be human together—to share the hard times and the happy, the struggles and the victories.

I realize eventually that the swing is gone, lost somewhere to time and nature. But I can always keep what I learned in that season. If I lean in and listen hard enough, it seems I can hear an echo from all the way back then. It's telling me to try less and trust more, to remember life is better when it's shared, to believe sweet chaos is sometimes just a sign that you're fully alive.

I walk home with dirt on the bottom of my shoes, sweat dripping down my neck, a bittersweet smile on my face. I feel grateful for then and now. And for all the folks who might be willing to join me for a sticky Popsicle (or, even better, a grown-up cup of coffee).

God, life is full of seasons we share with different people. Thank you for those who have shared our lives in the past, those who do so now, and even the folks we will connect with in the future. Amen.

• • • • •

Think of someone who made a difference in your life in the past. Reconnect with them in some small way today if possible or simply pause and enjoy remembering a moment you shared by recording it here.

LET'S BE UNEXPECTED WARRIORS, *love ninjas, secret agents of grace in the kitchens and the boardrooms and by the swings on the playground. They'll never see us coming.*

—Fiercehearted

EIGHTEEN

What Really Fits

Therefore, as God's chosen people, holy and dearly loved, clothe yourselves with compassion, kindness, humility, gentleness and patience.

Colossians 3:12

I borrowed my friend's strappy tank top. She lived in a fancy two-story house with a pool out back. Beside the pool was a tree house where we once played spin the bottle with neighborhood boys (I somehow found a way out of my turn). And between the pool and the tree house was hot cement that felt a bit like a rough cast-iron skillet when we laid our towels on it underneath the Texas sun.

This friend had dozens of trendy shirts. She held up the newest addition to her collection one day. Neon pink, orange, and lime green. Black geometric lines. We were children of the eighties. I coveted this shirt with a burning longing that felt like cinnamon candy in my throat. "Can I try it on?" I asked. "I don't know if it will work for you," she responded uncertainly. I paid no attention. I snatched it from her hands and retreated to the bathroom to change.

At twelve, this friend had bronze skin and curves like the Sahara desert. An endless summer of early hormones. I, on the other hand, was still all winter. Skin as white as Minnesota snow and a silhouette as flat as a frozen-over lake.

I knew this as soon as I put on that tank top. I knew it in my still-a-girl bones. But I could not accept it just then. Surely if I stuck out my chest far enough and pulled the straps tight, I could make it work.

That shirt, everything about it, was not meant for me. But I stepped out of the bathroom anyway. I wore it with self-consciousness and stubbornness, impressing no one, squirming in my skin. And, as luck would have it, I spilled something on it by the end of the day. Something dark and irremovable. The shirt not meant for me could now not be worn by my friend either.

After that day, she didn't invite me over as often. Eventually we drifted apart, and I would give her a half smile when we passed in the halls of junior high—she with her fellow desert sisters, boys occasionally whistling behind them.

I have always regretted that day. First, because I did not consider my friend when I all but stole her new shirt. But also because I told myself in that bathroom when I put it on, when I knew it didn't fit, that I must wear it anyway. It was the first time I did so, but it would not be the last.

I have worn the shirt of "outgoing" while my true nature begged for quiet.

I have worn the shirt of "I'm fine" when my heart was anything but.

I have worn the shirt of "cool girl" (or at least tried) when I really like warm so much better.

I did this for a long time. Until the straps cut into my shoulders. Until all I thought about was not letting anything slip out of place—how embarrassing. Until I sank down, exhausted, on the hot cement and said, "Jesus, I can't do this anymore." And he, with great gentleness and tenderness, came over and wrapped grace around my exposed places.

Then he walked me back inside and taught me what this means. "You have taken away my clothes of mourning and clothed me with joy" (Ps. 30:11 NLT). Perhaps these shirts weren't traditional mourning clothes, but in them I was always mourning who I was not—who I would never be.

Joy comes when we accept who we are, when we're true to who God made us. When we return the borrowed tank tops, the things that don't fit no matter how hard we try. When we stop living bare and uncertain. We, the fiercehearted, are covered by grace. We are created by God. We are "clothed with strength and dignity" (Prov. 31:25).

Joy comes when we accept who we are, when we're true to who God made us.

God, you say we're your creation, and you don't make mistakes. Give us eyes to see ourselves as you do, not to compare but instead to use all of who we are to bring you glory. Amen.

• • • • •

Pick an item from your closet, like a bracelet or scarf, to wear today. Each time you notice it, use it as a reminder to thank God again for making you who you are. What are three strengths he's given you? (If these are hard to come up with, ask someone who loves you.)

Jesus said we all must deny ourselves,

and perhaps this is part of what he meant. That at some point in our lives, we must give up trying to become someone he never intended us to be.

—*Fiercehearted*

NINETEEN

Telling

I praise you because I am fearfully and wonderfully made;
your works are wonderful,
I know that full well.

Psalm 139:14

I step into a junior high lunchroom that smells like old fries and sticky plastic trays. I scan the scene—the popular kids at one table, bookworms at another, the theater crowd and the athletes and the rebels. Who will look up and invite me over?

Tell me who I am.

My friends and I have crushes and dates and boyfriends. We fix our hair a hundred different ways. Crowd into dressing rooms to try on a thousand different outfits. Loop silver and gold through our ears. The doorbell rings and he is holding roses.

Tell me who I am.

I am typing into a small screen and pressing "publish." Sending my heart in black-and-white onto the internet. There will be comments and likes, criticisms and compliments. I watch the cursor blink.

Tell me who I am.

Isn't this the whisper of our hearts as women? The friends, the men, the crowd. They will tell us if we are okay. If we are worthy. If we are enough. Isn't that their job?

But then I bump into this verse: "But Jesus would not entrust himself to them, for he knew all people" (John 2:24). All people. The popular kids and the bookworms, the theater crowd and the athletes and the rebels. This verse has been there all along and it's been a head-scratcher for me. He didn't entrust himself to them?

Then suddenly it occurs to me that this might be the answer: Jesus is the only human to walk this spinning planet and not say, "Tell me who I am." He didn't look to others to define his identity or determine his worth. "Instead, he entrusted himself to him who judges justly" (1 Pet. 2:23). *Judge* has a reputation of being a harsh word, but I don't think that's the meaning here. I think it's saying that God alone knows the truest truth, and that's why his opinion is the only one that really matters.

Of course we're going to care what others think. We're going to desire acceptance and want to fit in. This is the way we're created to connect. The only folks who don't are sociopaths. So no guilt about this, no shame or hardening our hearts. Instead, we can simply say, "But God gets the final word."

Tell me who I am.

God says we are beloved and chosen, cherished and gifted, divinely created wonders. When someone says, "You'll never amount to anything," his Word says, "The Lord will work out his plans for my life" (Ps. 138:8 NLT). When someone tells us, "You don't look the right way," he whispers, "[You are] fearfully and wonderfully made" (Ps. 139:14). When someone implies, "You aren't wanted," he declares, "I have called you by name; you are mine" (Isa. 43:1 NLT).

God says we are beloved and chosen, cherished and gifted, divinely created wonders.

He is the One who gives us our identity. The One who sets us free from condemnation and comparison, hustling to be liked and trying to be perfect. The One right there with us every time we feel tempted to listen to the lies. May his love always be louder than any other voice.

God, tell us who we are.

God, you are the One who gets the final word on who we are. Your opinion matters more than the comments or the commercials, the latest trends or the expectations. On the days when it's hard to remember what's true, remind us of who we are in you. Amen.

• • • • •

Psalm 139:14 says we praise God when we understand how he's created us. Take a moment to praise him for who he's made you.

You are actually quite wonderful.

This isn't something you can see yet or anything you even feel most days. Have the courage to start believing it anyway, because contrary to what you fear, it will humble you. It will make you lift your hands in praise to the One who made you. And then extend those same hands to bless those around you.

—*Fiercehearted*

TWENTY

Arrows

But encourage one another daily, as long as it is called "Today," so that none of you may be hardened by sin's deceitfulness.

Hebrews 3:13

We gather in chairs around my dining room table. We go heart-deep, and one of my dear friends says, "I've struggled with believing the lie that I'm not smart enough." It's a stunning confession to those of us listening because, as another friend replies, "You're one of the smartest people I know!"

Later someone else admits she's struggled with believing she's not good enough. And we are again shocked because she's a woman of faithfulness and excellence in our eyes. I add my own lie, that I have strived to earn my worth because I sometimes don't believe who I am is adequate. Yet I'm the girl God has used to write books about embracing who we are and becoming all God created us to be.

A light bulb comes on as I realize that the enemy is lying to us in areas related to our giftings.

I imagine he does the same with you. Because I think the purpose of the lie is to hold us back from who we're made to be and what we're called to do. These attacks are startling, but we need to acknowledge that they're a normal part of life as a believer, soldier, and fighter. And they will be until we're in heaven.

We've already come so far in our journey together on these pages. But before we take another step, I want to say one more time that we will still have battles to fight. Yes, we may have times when it feels like the lies have been fully defeated. But then they come back, and if we don't understand the reality of what's happening, we can feel a lot of shame and guilt. We can wonder, *What is wrong with me?*

I was praying about that one day, and I felt like the Lord showed me that all it means when we hear those lies again is that we're still at war because we're still living in a fallen world. If we're soldiers on a battlefield and someone is shooting arrows at us, is that a reason to be ashamed? Is that a reason to feel guilty? *No!*

That is a reason to say, "You know what? I am a warrior! I have fought hard and I'm going to *keep* fighting hard. I'm doing what my Commanding Officer has called me to do, which is to stand my ground and never stop fighting."

So if we are in a battle today or tomorrow or a decade from now, and if we hear lies, let's not allow the enemy to shame us or make us feel guilty.

Instead, let's block those arrows and say, "No, in Jesus's name, I'm a warrior and I'm going to resist until the day I go home."

We are stronger and braver together.

At times we will need our sisters to lock shields with us, too, and say, "I'm going to take those arrows for a while. I'm going to stand in the gap for you." There is no shame in that either. In the kingdom of God, there is no such thing as an army of one.

We are stronger and braver together.

God, you understand that to live in this world means to be at war. You experienced it firsthand. Thank you for giving us the strength to keep fighting, the bravery to never give up or give in, and the truth we can stand on always. With you we will not be defeated. Amen.

• • • • •

Think of a time when you faced a battle in your life. What helped you achieve victory? Recall those things so you can be prepared when you need them again.

THERE IS NO SHAME *in being a warrior. Fight on.*

—Fiercehearted

TWENTY-ONE

Opposition and Opportunity

I will stay on . . . because a great door for effective work has opened to me, and there are many who oppose me.

1 Corinthians 16:8–9

Just between you and me, sometimes when I read the Bible, it sounds like the apostle Paul is out of his ever-lovin' mind. I imagine getting to heaven and saying to him, "Paul, man, some of that stuff you wrote. Whew." Then we'd have a good laugh about it because, of course, it's really me who needs to learn to see things differently.

For example, when I read these words the other morning, I thought my Bible must have a typo or the translators had eaten too much pizza the night before. First Corinthians 16:8–9 says, "I will stay on . . . because a great door for effective work has opened to me, and there are many who oppose me."

The Holley Gerth version would read, "I'm getting out of here because there's a lot of opposition and surely that means God has closed the door." Anyone else with me?

But, no, Paul was looking at opposition as affirmation and confirmation. He was where he needed to be, doing what he needed to do. It was not a reason to give up or feel like a failure, to think he must have misheard God or be doing it wrong. Just the opposite: he decided this meant he should carry on.

We will all get to the place where we face "opposition" in God's will for our lives. Maybe it will come from within—the lies in our hearts will grow so loud that we'll be tempted to listen. Or perhaps the critics and naysayers and committees on the outside will do that work for us. It will be their voices we hear.

We will hang our heads, and in that moment the most natural, human thing in the world to say is, "I'm walking away. I've clearly messed this up." But perhaps Jesus is whispering, "Stay . . . a great door for effective work has opened to you, and there are many who oppose you." He understands this, after all. He faced opposition and resistance at every step.

If we find ourselves in the middle of blood and sweat and tears today, then we can remember this doesn't mean we're failing; it means we're fighting.

Sometimes what looks like opposition turns out to be an opportunity. It's an indication that it's time to press in, press on, and refuse to give up. It's a message that says we are fighting a worthwhile battle. It's proof that we are making a difference.

If we find ourselves in the middle of blood and sweat and tears today, then we can remember this doesn't mean we're failing; it means we're fighting. The enemy of our hearts knows the only way he can beat us is if he can convince us to retreat, to forfeit. If we stand firm, we can't lose. We'll never be defeated. We won't be overcome.

Here's the crazy secret the apostle Paul knew: with God, we've already won.

God, you understand what it is to face opposition in this world. You spent thirty-three years here. You also know how to overcome and turn those challenges into opportunities. Please show us how to do the same today. Amen.

· · · · ·

What feels like opposition in your life today? What's one way it might also be an opportunity? This opposition is giving me the opportunity to . . .

YOU'RE AN OVERCOMER. *You're loved. You're going to win. Keep fighting, brave and beautiful soul.*

—Fiercehearted

TWENTY-TWO

Blood on My Shirt

I can do all this through him who gives me strength.

Philippians 4:13

I come home with blood on my shirt. A single speck, the size of the end of a pin, and a smear the shape of a tiny moon. I throw the shirt in the washer but can't bring myself to push the start button. Instead, I stare at the stains, mystified and overcome.

I recall being at the bedside of my daughter, her face contorted with pain. Her left leg is in the crook of my right elbow. Her husband is on her other side, same position, like a mirror image. A doctor is between us and she calls out, "Push!" My daughter pulls on the end of a white knotted sheet, the other end held by her friend who is also a doula.

It is a merciless tug-of-war, Lovelle's face flushed with agony and the wild strength of a lioness. We count through the contraction. She leans back again, her head on the pillow, hair splayed all around her like a mane. She has never looked more beautiful to me.

In the pause, I think of words sent to me just last weekend, entirely out of the blue, by someone who knew my grandpa Hollie. She tells me how much he loved me, how proud he was of me, and she ends her note with this: "All of this to say, if you ever get discouraged, writer's block, etc., just know you're being cheered on! You're being cheered on by a great cloud of witnesses that includes your grandparents. So on behalf of Brother Hollie, keep running the race. You're making a difference."

She is quoting Hebrews 12:1, which says, "Since we are surrounded by so great a cloud of witnesses . . . let us run with endurance the race that is set before us" (NKJV). She doesn't know this is my life passage, the place I return to again and again when it feels like I can't take another step. She doesn't know that she has spoken exactly what I needed the weekend before I am to become a grandparent myself.

My thoughts are broken by the doctor's voice. "Push!" My daughter strains and we shout. I tell her over and over again, "You can do this! You *are* doing this. You are strong. You are brave." We are the great cloud of witnesses in this moment. Then the doctor is holding a baby and we are whooping and weeping. My granddaughter, Eula Ellen, is here. I am in awe. I am in love. I am witness to a miracle.

You can do this!
You *are* doing this.
You are strong.
You are brave.

I lean over my daughter, brush the matted hair back from her forehead. The sweat of her labor and salt of my tears run together like a tiny river onto the white sheet. The scenes of our story flash before me: Almost a decade of infertility for me, over two decades of hardship for her, almost four years since God unexpectedly brought us together as mother and daughter when she was twenty-one, and exactly three years to the day since we officially became a family.

I may have never experienced physically giving birth, but there is something in the laboring I understand in my bones. The pushing through the pain and tears and exhaustion, and the temptation to give up hope. Perhaps that's why I'm reluctant to wash away the stains on my shirt. They feel like holy reminders, like badges of honor.

I hold my granddaughter for the first time the next day. I put my cheek against hers, breathe in her skin, whisper to her that she is loved and strong and she is going to grow up to be a fiercehearted woman.

The great cloud of witnesses watches.

I can almost hear the cheers.

God, you know how hard it can be to live in this world. You've walked in our shoes. That means we can fix our eyes on you, follow you, and know you will get us through whatever we face. Give us endurance, hope, and faith every step of the way. Amen.

• • • • •

Think of a moment in your life when you felt like giving up but pushed through instead. What can you remember from that moment that can help you today?

The sorrow and the longing

and the joy are light and dark threads . . . woven together in ways only God could have fashioned.

—*Fiercehearted*

TWENTY-THREE

Secrets, Struggles, Scandalous Love

Who will bring any charge against those whom God has chosen? It is God who justifies. Who then is the one who condemns? No one.

Romans 8:33–34

On a recent evening, my daughter and I met for a writing date. We spread our laptops out on a wood-topped table in a corner booth of our favorite place. We ate delicious soup and clicked on our keyboards.

In between paragraphs we'd talk, and at some point our conversation drifted to an area in which I've personally struggled. I'd never shared this with her and I felt afraid about doing so.

I'm supposed to be her mama, after all. What if this made her feel unsure of me, unsafe in some way? But it seemed God kept nudging, so I cleared my throat and said, "There have been times in my life when this thing we're talking about has been a struggle for me."

She looked at me and said, without hesitation, "It helps to know you have struggles too." It felt like she handed me a piece of freedom my heart hungered for, like passing a bite of crusty bread across the table. Because don't we all do this? We tell ourselves that to be a helpful example we must be a flawless one. But this has never been the way, what our people really need.

Then I said, "We don't have secrets in our family. I want you to know that there is nothing you could ever tell me that would make me love you less. You can come to me with anything and there will never be any judgment. And if you feel like anything in your life is ever coming after you, I will stand with you and we will fight it together."

As those words came out of my mouth, it suddenly seemed like that corner booth became holy ground. Because I understood in a way I never had before what this means: "There is no condemnation for those who belong to Christ Jesus" (Rom. 8:1 NLT) and "If God is for us, who can ever be against us?" (Rom. 8:31 NLT).

What I said to my daughter our heavenly Father says to us today, right here and now: "We don't have secrets in our family. I want you to know that there is nothing you could ever tell me that would make me love you less. You can come to me with anything and there will never be any judgment. And if you feel like anything in your life is ever coming after you, I will stand with you and we will fight it together."

> The love of God for us and the grace of God toward us will never, ever change.

I know this is true in a deeper way than ever before, and I hope my daughter and my granddaughter and all my sisters like you know it too: *Whatever we did yesterday, whatever we're battling today, whatever we may face tomorrow, the love of God for us and the grace of God toward us will never, ever change.*

God, you are the grace-giver, the struggle-defeater, the victory-bringer. We will never face anything alone, not even our deepest, darkest secrets. You are with and for us always. Amen.

.....

What struggle are you facing right now? Dare to speak it first to God here and then consider sharing it with someone trustworthy who will pray for you and encourage you. Ask how you can pray for and encourage them too.

I TOLD THE TRUTH *about some things I'd rather keep hidden under the couch cushions with the dirty pennies. I admitted to both struggles and victories. I didn't make so many statements. I told more stories. This felt wild and scandalous to me. Vulnerable and beautiful.*

—Fiercehearted

TWENTY-FOUR

Intimacy, Not Intimidation

A new command I give you: Love one another. As I have loved you, so you must love one another. By this everyone will know that you are my disciples, if you love one another.

John 13:34–35

Two friends and I stand under a lovely early evening sky. We've just come from a gathering of women, the kind that is both wonderful and vulnerable at the same time. "That was intimidating," one of us says.

We all nod in agreement. Then we talk about how this happens, how we can be with people we like and admire and hold dear, and then all of a sudden the enemy is whispering lies in our ears.

My signature lie is "You're not good enough." When I hear this, my mind startles like a thoroughbred racehorse. My thoughts are out of the gate before I even fully realize what's happening. I need to try harder. I need to do more. The staccato sentences pound like hooves against a track.

When I confess this out loud to my two friends, I find, of course, I'm not the only one. Perhaps you've experienced something similar too. "What do we do about this?" our little group asks each other. Then suddenly I say something that has never occurred to me before in all my years on this spinning earth (when that happens, I tend to think Jesus has something to do with it).

"I think the cure for intimidation is intimacy."

We first need intimacy with Jesus because he is the One whose voice tells us who we really are, who we're created to be, what's true of us no matter how we feel in any given moment. *He says we are loved and chosen, wonderfully made and part of his plan.*

Then we need intimacy with others—safe places where we can say to each other, "I don't have it all together." We are all more alike than different. We are all broken and beloved daughters in need of a Savior.

And we need intimacy with our own hearts too. *Because when we don't take time to discover who we are, we feel a lot of pressure to be someone else.*

We are all more alike than different. We are all broken and beloved daughters in need of a Savior.

Next time I feel insecure, I'm going to pause and ask myself, *How can I choose intimacy instead of intimidation right now?* I can type that, and it sounds so spiritual and mature, but I will likely be (a) hiding under a table, (b) eating too many cookies in an attempt to calm myself down, (c) making a face like a crazed monkey in a social situation where that's not appropriate, or (d) all of the above.

That conversation on a spring evening with my friends felt like a start to something freeing and new. So in case you've ever felt like me, I wanted to pass it along to you. Let's reject the intimidation that can keep us apart and instead embrace the grace that draws us together in Jesus.

God, you never meant for us to go through life alone. Yet it's so easy to live that way, even when we're in a crowd. Give us the courage to connect, to love like you do, to trade intimidation for intimacy. Amen.

. . . . .

Think of a relationship or situation where it's tempting to let intimidation get the best of you. What's one truth you could say to yourself in that moment to help give you the courage to move toward intimacy instead?

I WANT TO LOOK BEYOND *my preferences and admirations, my insecurities and assumptions, my appraisals and fears. I want to stop asking, "How does this person see me?" and instead understand, "How can I really see them?"*

—Fiercehearted

TWENTY-FIVE

Threats, Promises

The Lord is my strength and my defense;
he has become my salvation.
Shouts of joy and victory
resound in the tents of the righteous:
"The Lord's right hand has done mighty things!"

Psalm 118:14–15

A friend of mine and I talked about hard times in our lives. We traded battle stories over salads, forks in our hands like weapons. We pondered how when things get tough in our lives the enemy seems to look for chances to do even more damage—to divide, bring discouragement, whisper lies. *Have you ever experienced this too?*

In other words, the enemy of our hearts is an opportunist. "Your enemy the devil prowls around like a roaring lion looking for someone to devour" (1 Pet. 5:8). We need to know this so we can be on guard, so we can fight for, rather than against, our own hearts and each other.

As my friend and I talked more, we realized something else, too, something that felt ancient and yet new. God is also an opportunist. "God causes everything to work together for the good of those who love God and are called according to his purpose for them" (Rom. 8:28 NLT).

When things get tough in our lives, God looks for a chance to do even more good to and for us—*to unite, bring hope, whisper truth*. We need to know this so we can look for what he wants to offer our hearts, the treasures hidden in the darkness, the unexpected spoils of war.

Not long before this conversation with my friend, my mom had underwent heart surgery. She had gone in for a routine test, which led to a blockage being found, which turned into emergency triple bypass surgery, followed by a three-week hospital stay filled with complications and scary moments. As I sat by my mom's bed, walked the hospital halls, and prayed desperately, it sometimes seemed I could feel the breath of the enemy on my neck, ready to devour. But, even more, I could sense the presence of Jesus, *the Lion of Judah* (Rev. 5:5) walking with me, roaring for our family, giving us what we needed most in that hard place.

My mama is home now and regaining her strength. That experience with her reminded me again that we are humans on a broken, uncertain earth. We are warriors disguised in tennis shoes and yoga pants. We bleed and cry and drink cups of bitter hospital coffee. We are small and yet part of a bigger, wilder story than we can even imagine, one that's been unfolding since the beginning of time.

We are warriors disguised in tennis shoes and yoga pants.

Today the enemy of our hearts is working in our lives.

Today the God of all eternity is working in our lives.

I don't think I have to tell you which one is going to win, which one has already won. God lets no threat go undefeated. He lets no opportunity in our lives be wasted. He is mighty, invincible, and relentless in his love for us.

God, you are always working in our lives and turning what seem like threats into opportunities. You are stronger than anything that comes against us. Give us your protection and fulfill your purposes for us today. Amen.

· · · · ·

What feels like a threat in your life today, a place where you're experiencing fear or uncertainty? What's one way you can see God working in that circumstance or situation?

AS THE SAYING GOES, *"Be kind, for everyone you meet is fighting a hard battle." This happens to be mine. I know my enemy's name now. And I am not afraid to say it out loud. Whatever you're facing today, you don't need to hide or hang your head either.*

—Fiercehearted

TWENTY-SIX

Accept the Gifts

Whatever is good and perfect is a gift coming down to us from God our Father, who created all the lights in the heavens. He never changes or casts a shifting shadow.

James 1:17 NLT

My grandmother is sitting at my kitchen table, the one worn smooth from years and many hands, the heat of casserole dishes and the rough edges of silverware. It's the same table my husband ate at in his childhood, so it seems a fitting setting for this conversation. I open a small book filled with questions about spiritual legacy, press record on the memo feature of my phone, and invite my grandma to give voice to her history.

We start with what I know—that she was born in a little southern town, married my grandpa at age fifteen, dropped out of high school, worked in a cookie factory, had two kids before she blew out the candles on her twenty-first birthday cake. I know also that life was hard and that while the name of Jesus was present in her home, faith wasn't always deeply personal for her. That came later, in her twenties, when a neighbor kept inviting her to church and she went. She decided, once and for all, that she would follow the God who kept so tenderly pursuing her. She became a youth director (nicknamed

"Brother Eula" because she was the first woman in the church to hold the position). She would later work at a children's home and eventually teach high school (the two grades she missed when she dropped out). Now almost ninety years old, she's led the same Sunday school class for over thirty years and teaches a Bible study at the local nursing home once a week.

I know these things, yet I love to hear her tell them again. I love the reciting of the stories and the way she smiles when she gets to the part about me, her oldest grandchild, being born. What I don't know is what she would say to me now, a granddaughter in her fortieth year on this spinning planet. "What do you wish someone had told you when you were forty?" I ask. She pauses for a long time—you can hear it in the recording—and then she says, simply and thoughtfully, "Accept God's gifts with gladness."

She knows me well—that I'm prone to placing pressure on myself, to wrestling with guilt and fear, to making burdens out of blessings. When she leaves, I kiss her on the cheek and she smells like my childhood, like something safe and good. After she's gone, I can't stop thinking about what she said. I think of it when the sun reaches its fingers into the bedroom of our new house. I think of it when an unexpected opportunity waltzes into my inbox. I think of it when my to-do list is long and my patience is short. *Accept God's gifts with gladness.*

The world rests not on our shoulders but in God's hands.

I think accepting God's gifts with gladness is ultimately about humility. It's remembering to say thank you more often. It's understanding that the world rests not on our shoulders but in God's hands. It's daring to experience the most vulnerable of emotions—happiness, delight, freedom. It's living with open hands rather than clenching them in fear or striving. It's having the courage to not let the enemy of our hearts steal the joy of what's ours.

I have a picture of my grandma and me on a shelf in our living room. It's Easter and we are both wearing fancy dresses. I am in the awkward season of life with gangly legs and home-cut bangs. My grandmother is smiling, her arm around me, the hem of her dress caught by the wind. Life had been hard for her, I know, but in this moment it doesn't show. She looks instead like God has been good to her, like she's a kid at a birthday party who's just pulled the lid off another present, like she knows a secret she's willing to tell.

God, you give us so much every day. We are surrounded by your goodness. We ask for eyes to see what is from your hand and hearts that respond with thanks. Grant us the courage to choose joy and gratitude. Amen.

• • • • •

What's a gift from God in your life that you're sometimes tempted to treat as a burden? Pause and tell him thank you for it today.

The little gifts and tiny moments . . .

lead us, like bread crumbs, back to the feet of the Maker of all. "Oh, there you are," we say to him. "This is not where I was expecting to find you." And I think perhaps he smiles and says, "Ah yes, but I've been here all along."

—Fiercehearted

TWENTY-SEVEN

Under Wings

He will cover you with his feathers,
and under his wings you will find refuge;
his faithfulness will be your shield and rampart.

Psalm 91:4

We live in a spotlight-seeking world. Get on the stage. Post the status update. Build the platform. Do the *big* things. But so much of life is the opposite. It's the laundry tumbling in the dryer, the making of dinner, the washing of little hands. It's the reports silently completed and filed away. It's encouraging words spoken over coffee to a hurting friend. It's the unrecognized and unacknowledged and uncelebrated. Most of life doesn't feel like the spotlight; it feels like the shadows.

This can make our hearts feel as if we are somehow falling short of our purpose. Perhaps we are even disappointing God. I pondered this on a recent walk around our neighborhood. It might seem as if I have a very public job, but a surprising amount of my time consists of me sitting in front of a laptop with nothing but a mug of coffee for a companion. There are moments when I look around and it seems that everyone else is doing more—and doing it better and faster. I start feeling like I need to hustle. I need to try harder. I am in everyone else's shadow.

Under Wings

Last year a robin settled down just outside our guest bathroom window in a place where we could watch the whole process unfold. I know from that experience that new birds spend a good bit of time under the wings of their parents. As I walked and looked at the nests tucked into leafy branches and guarded by robins and sparrows, I wondered if their little ones were under their wings too.

Then I remembered what the psalmist wrote: "How priceless is your unfailing love, O God! People take refuge in the shadow of your wings" (Ps. 36:7). I suddenly realized this: *when we feel we are in the shadows, we are actually in the shadow of God's wings.* This is a place of protection and grace, of affection and care. "Have mercy on me, my God, have mercy on me, for in you I take refuge. I will take refuge in the shadow of your wings until the disaster has passed" (Ps. 57:1).

When we feel we are in the shadows, we are actually in the shadow of God's wings.

When we feel unnoticed, when we're tempted to compare, we can reassure our hearts with this truth: *we are never in anyone's shadow but God's.* This means the moments or seasons when we seem to be in the shadows are not failures or disappointments. They are gifts from God.

This world tells us to seek the spotlight. But David, a man after God's own heart, prayed for the opposite: "Keep me as the apple of your eye; hide me in the shadow of your wings" (Ps. 17:8). Yes, he would have very public moments of giant-slaying, nation-leading, and battle-winning, but it seemed he recognized the value of being hidden in God. All our hearts need a place to remember who we are, find peace and rest, and be covered by the One who loves us most of all.

"Because you are my help, I sing in the shadow of your wings" (Ps. 63:7). These words are beautiful to me because they are about offering our hearts for an audience of one. In the shadow of God's wings, life isn't about performance; it's about praise. It's not about proving our worth; it's about sharing our gratefulness. It's not about gaining attention; it's about dwelling in the affection of the One who keeps us in the place we most need to be—under his wings, close to his heart.

God, you cover us, you care for us, you keep us close to your heart, and there is no better place in all the world to be. We choose to remain where you've placed us, to believe our worth comes always and only from being seen and known and loved by you. Amen.

• • • • •

Every time you see a bird today, let it be a reminder that you are under God's wings and in his care. Pause now and take a moment to tell him "Thank you" or "I love you" or "I trust you see me."

This is what I wish for her,

this woman sitting across from me, that God will do in her life what he did in mine—rescue her from herself and her desires. That he will speak to her under starry night skies and guard her when the spotlight is so bright it threatens to sunburn her soul.

—*Fiercehearted*

TWENTY-EIGHT

Pink Hair

She is clothed with strength and dignity,
and she laughs without fear of the future.
Proverbs 31:25 NLT

She wanted pink hair, just a little on the right side. A tiny piece of art shaved into the fine blonde hairs just above the nape of her neck like a secret only she could decide when to share. This was her birthday present. I watched this ten-year-old perched in a stylist's chair while I waited for my appointment. She had blue eyes like the start of a summer evening, a swirl of innocence and mischief.

The pink dye would wash out, the faint design quickly become overgrown like an unmowed lawn. But I sensed something in this girl's bones, a tender kind of strength and bravery that would intensify in the years to come.

This generation coming up, they know so much sooner than I did that there is a part of them meant to be a warrior. I remember standing for a baby dedication at church recently, listening to the names and meanings of the little ones. I noted a common thread—words like *strong, fighter, victorious*. These girl babies—nestled in cotton and fluff, cheeks like just-picked peaches—looked around curiously from their mothers' arms. I thought of how the names and the bearers of them seemed like a paradox. Because for so long we've been told to choose. Be tough or tender. Be strong or soft. Be kind or courageous. But we missed the point: the choice has never been either/or. In this hard world, tender is tough. Soft is strong. Courageous is kind. Why? Because this is the nature of God. And we are created in his image.

Tender is tough.
Soft is strong.
Courageous is kind.

Oh, yes, we grow beyond the baby stage. We become girls and then women. But sometimes we give up so much along the way that we don't have to. I want to be a woman who helps this next generation embrace all the parts of who they are. I don't want them to make the mistakes I did, believe the lies I have, get wounded in the ways I've experienced.

When the ten-year-old girl got up from the stylist's chair, I could read just one word on her T-shirt, *strong*. I said, "I like your hair. What does the rest of your shirt say?" She uncrossed her arms. "Strong Like Mom." Ah, yes.

I'm not up for a wild color or shaved art on the back of my head just yet. I got a trim and plain ol' highlights when it was my turn in the stylist's chair. But I want to take my place now as a fiercehearted woman because there are others coming after me like a wild and lovely parade—the little sisters and the daughters and the pink-haired granddaughters.

God, you are our Creator. You made us women and this is a beautiful, powerful thing. We have never been an afterthought; we have always been an essential part of your plan. We are your beloved daughters and we want to bring you glory in this generation. Amen.

. . . . .

Think of a younger woman in your life. Encourage her in some way today or take a moment to write a prayer for her here.

IMAGINE THE SCENE [IN EDEN]. . . . *A hush comes as the Artist begins to work. He stretches the rib out long and adds curves and flesh and eyelashes. Yes, a freckle just above her lip, a wrinkle on her elbow, a softness in the palms of her hands, and a strength between her shoulder blades. I think God smiles.*

—Fiercehearted

TWENTY-NINE

Walk by Faith

See how very much our Father loves us, for he calls us his children, and that is what we are!

1 John 3:1 NLT

My granddaughter, Ellie, is learning to walk. She clings to whatever surface she can find—the edge of a table, the leg of a chair, and, most of all, the hands of those who love her. We hold her up and we help her take one wobbly step after another. When she manages to make a bit of progress, we cheer. When she loses her balance and lands on her bottom, we tell her to try again. We are her biggest fans, her strongest supporters, the ones who will not let go.

I've been thinking of this lately because I feel a bit wobbly on the inside. The progress I'm making doesn't feel smooth or sure. It feels slow and awkward. I worry so often, *What if God is disappointed in me?* When this question comes to mind, I freeze. It seems too risky to take another step because it might be wrong. *I will wait,* I tell myself, *until I know that I can make everything work out the way I hope.* I want to be sure I won't fall.

But Ellie is teaching me this is not the way it's meant to go. She's so much wiser than me in many ways. She doesn't fear that she'll lose our approval if she messes up. More often than not she laughs when her diaper-padded backside hits the ground. She doesn't think we love her because of how many steps she takes. She doesn't feel the need (yet) for independence—to prove she can do it on her own. Instead, she's quite giddy to have all the help she can get. She reminds me all over again what it means to have childlike faith.

"About that time the disciples came to Jesus and asked, 'Who is greatest in the Kingdom of Heaven?' Jesus called a little child to him and put the child among them. Then he said, 'I tell you the truth, unless you turn from your sins and become like little children, you will never get into the Kingdom of Heaven. So anyone who becomes as humble as this little child is the greatest in the Kingdom of Heaven'" (Matt. 18:1–4 NLT).

This is the paradox I so often miss: Bravery doesn't come from bravado. It comes from humility. I so often want to impress God when what he wants most is for me to place my hand in his. I can think I'm so much bigger and stronger than I am, than he's asking me to be. Our culture says independence is the ultimate goal, that we're to pull ourselves up by our own bootstraps. But Jesus said the one who is greatest is the one who is the most dependent, the one who knows God alone supports and sustains her. Because when we depend on him, we have access to all his strength and power, all his might and goodness.

By the time you read these words Ellie will be running circles around the living room, chasing the dog, and jumping on the bed. This is how it's meant to be. But it's different for our hearts. We never have to stand alone. We never have to take the next step by ourselves. We never outgrow our need for a God who holds us up, who cheers us on, who never lets us go.

We never outgrow our need for a God who holds us up, who cheers us on, who never lets us go.

God, we are your children and we never have to take a single step on our own. When we forget that's true, draw us close and help us cling to you. We are yours. We are loved. That's all that really matters. Amen.

• • • • •

Think of a child in your life. What's one thing they show you about what it means to have childlike faith?

MAYBE THE LITTLE GIRL *who twirls in her grape-juice-splattered skirt and holler-sings "Jesus loves me, this I know, for the Bible tells me so" is really so much wiser than I am with all my respectable lessons and learning. Maybe this is another example of what Jesus meant when he told us to have childlike faith. Not faith that completely understands but faith that trusts.*

—Fiercehearted

THIRTY

Not Getting It Right

That is why, for Christ's sake, I delight in weaknesses, in insults, in hardships, in persecutions, in difficulties. For when I am weak, then I am strong.

2 Corinthians 12:10

I pull into a parking lot near the studio on a summer Tuesday. A few minutes early, I watch children on a playground, hair matted with sweat, shoes untied, dirt on their knees. I wish I could breathe in some of their intoxicating enthusiasm and restlessness. Instead, I grab my purse and tea and walk inside like a maiden going down the plank of a pirate ship, hoping the waters are shallower than they look and the sharks are away on vacation.

Inside I'm greeted by a kind face. "Are you Holley?" I nod in affirmation, the idea of denying my identity a fleeting thought, like a sparrow swooping across my mind. I'm guided to a small room with padding on the walls. I'm here to record the audiobook of *Fiercehearted*.

I recognize the irony—a book about courage and grit, yet I stand here with knees knocking. But I've also come to understand this is the fiercehearted way. We do it afraid.

So I take a seat in a surprisingly cozy chair. A microphone is scooted close to my mouth. I read the copyright information of the book aloud over and over again while levels and volumes and details beyond my scope of understanding are checked by experts I feel so grateful for in this moment.

Then it's time.

I begin to read words I wrote in the dark on a plane as I sniffled into a too-small napkin and tried not to scare my seatmate. Others I typed in a coffee shop with white brick walls, graffiti scratched into the surface. The ones that woke me in the night and in the day, in the heart way. It feels vulnerable to say these things out loud, to actually release them into the universe where they will float around with Wi-Fi signals and cell phone calls and the war songs of birds.

I find I can't say certain phrases well, like femininity and Parmigiano Reggiano. I laugh when I'm not supposed to and I swallow too hard and too often. But we, the patient producer and I, make it to the very last piece. It is in this moment when I can see the finish line, when I can imagine the clicking off of the microphone and the reprieve from my own voice, that my stomach decides to stage a coup.

All of a sudden a roar like a primitive beast comes from my midsection. I begin to sweat—could anyone hear that? The producer asks through my headphones, "Um, was that your stomach?" I tell the truth. I see his grin through the glass between us. "Try it again," he says.

But the beast wants snacks and protests. Good grief. Self-sabotage of the most embarrassing sort. A few more tries and we finally get it. I finish with my arms folded across me as a muffler. When we're done, the producer says, "Great job. Go get something to eat." I walk back to the car where the children have finished their playing and I think of their matted, sweaty hair and the dirt on their knees again. Why is it that we, as grown-ups, are so humbled when it becomes apparent we're human?

Maybe the beast was more than hungry; maybe it was wise. Maybe what I heard wasn't a demand but a reminder not to take myself so seriously. Perhaps it was not meant as rebellion or a rebuke but more like the ringing of a freedom bell deep inside me.

Life is not about getting it right the first time.

This is what children and the fiercehearted know and embrace, what grown-ups can ignore and forget: life is not about getting it right the first time.

God, it can be tempting to believe if we're not perfect, then somehow we're letting you down. But it's often in our weakness, in our failures and humanness that you are mysteriously lifted up. Give us the courage to show up as we are, trusting that your grace is enough and you will get your glory from every part of our stories. Amen.

• • • • •

Is there anything in your life that you've avoided because you're afraid it might not go well? If so, write it here and consider giving it a try anyway.

I am the belly flopper

and star performer, mess and perfectionist, struggler and self-sufficient desperado. I am paradox and contradiction, contrast and inconsistency.

—*Fiercehearted*

THIRTY-ONE

Take the Grace

God's grace has made me what I am, and his grace to me was not wasted.

1 Corinthians 15:10 NCV

I am an accidental jabber, an elbow swinger, the points in my joints like two miniature wrecking balls. Just this morning my left elbow bumped into a white coffee mug with foam swirled in its center. I watched in slow motion as my latte spilled like a muddy brown river down the slate countertop and dripped toward the floor, a caffeinated Niagara.

This event felt disproportionately epic to me, worthy of an environmental cleanup team and news cameras, or at least the attention of every customer. But when I looked up, no one had even noticed. I shuffled to the bar and cleared my throat at a guy half my age. Because I am so smooth, I said, "Itotallyspilledmycoffee." I gushed it just like that, one big word, one breath, because I'm nervous and inordinately ashamed. I blurted it like I was confessing my darkest secret to a priest in a confessional box.

He tilted his head full of brown curls to the side and he offered an amused smile. I asked for a rag, so he grabbed one but refused to turn it over. "Where?" he asked and followed me to the carnage, then proceeded to clean up every bit of my mess. When he was done, he lifted my mug. "What did you have?" I gave an answer. "I'll have them make you another," he said, and before I could protest or offer to pay, he was gone, stained rag swishing like a happy dog's tail next to his ripped jeans.

A few moments later, the barista hollered, "Holley!" and it was as if I was in a time machine. I'd pressed the button and was back to the beginning, back to the place before the clumsy elbows and the flood. As I claimed my new drink, I realized this whole scenario felt familiar, as if I've somehow lived it a thousand times before.

I thought then of all the moments fear had knocked my courage right over and I didn't have a drop of it left. But then Jesus, so kind, got the rag and mopped it up. Then he gave me another cup and said, "Try again." This is what he does for me, and for you, always.

Jesus will never run out of grace. And we will never run out of reasons we need it.

We are all clumsy with faith. We are messy with love. We are awkward with doing what God has asked of us. There is no way around this. It's the way of humans in this world. Knowing this can paralyze us if we believe this means we must be perfect. Or it can free us if we let it show us we need a Savior. Let's choose the latter. Let's take the mercy and the forgiveness and the million second chances.

Jesus will never run out of grace.

And we will never run out of reasons we need it.

God, we need your grace every single moment, every single day, every single breath. We gratefully receive it and ask that you help us pass it on to others who need it too. Thank you that there will always be more than enough for all of us. Amen.

• • • • •

Who needs extra grace in your life today?
What's one way you can give it to them?

We are all more alike than different.

We are all broken. We are all beautiful.

We are all in need of grace.

—*Fiercehearted*

THIRTY-TWO

Broken, Beautiful

We know that in all things God works for the good of those who love him, who have been called according to his purpose.

Romans 8:28

My daughter stands over the sink, wet pan in her hands, bubbles across her fingertips, and words spilling out of her mouth like water from the faucet. Then a clank and the sound of shattering. Pieces, pieces everywhere. Clear glass on the countertops and in the fruit basket and on the tops of our feet. We freeze, shocked, and I watch her eyes grow wide. Then she throws her head back and laughs.

That laughter sounds like a thousand church bells. It sounds like waves in the ocean and wind in the trees and the pour of hot chocolate into a cup on a cold day. "Are you okay?" I ask her. She nods and I think, *Oh, yes. Yes, you really are.*

Then my husband comes running at the noise and we are a family on our knees together, searching for shards in corners, beneath the refrigerator, and glinting from the grout between the tiles. Most of the pieces are big—the sizes of dimes and nickels. And at some point I suddenly realize they are beautiful, that all this brokenness scattered everywhere is catching the light in strange, gorgeous ways. I find myself saying, "I could make something of this." I picture a mosaic tabletop, a picture frame, hot glue, and some kind of cement.

I realize then, in that very moment, that we can see life as a series of obstacles or invitations. Choosing the laughter means looking at whatever is in front of us and saying, "I could make something of this." Or, more accurately, "God could make something of this." It's not giving in to the fear. It's not throwing in the trash the parts of us that seem unusable or unworthy. It's seeing the lovely in the most unlikely places. And, yes, we're inevitably going to get some scratches on our hands. We'll likely bleed a bit along the way and search the back of the cabinets for Band-Aids. We'll be frustrated and unsure, sometimes sad or disappointed. We'll wonder if it could have turned out differently or if maybe we could have done it all better. But in the end, we'll give ourselves over to what is, who we are, and our mysterious God.

I know this all over again as I look up at my daughter who's now leaning on the edge of the counter, looking a little tentative. She's worried about the mess she's caused. I walk over to her and put my arm around her shoulders.

"We love you," I say. "All is well," I reassure.

We are broken.
We are beautiful.
We are beloved.

What if that's how it is with God too? What if we are the ones with the pans in our hands and the best of intentions in our hearts? The ones trying so hard and having it all slip out of our grasp anyway. The ones who watch our plans shatter and our attempts to be perfect crash. And God is offering us this: to know we are safe and loved and allowed to be human.

We are broken. We are beautiful. We are beloved.

God, we entrust our brokenness to you. We give you all the pieces of our lives. We trust you to make them into something whole. On the days when we can't see that, when we don't feel it, when it's hard to keep believing, give us the hope and strength we need. Amen.

• • • • •

As you go through your day, look for broken pieces—mosaics, stained glass, bits of a cookie crumbled on top of ice cream. Each time you see some, let them be a reminder of how God is working all things together for good even in the broken parts of our lives. What brokenness do you have in your life right now? How is God working in it?

WHAT WE SO OFTEN NEED *is not a big break but to be broken. To come to the place where we are disappointed by all we've been chasing, when we're humbled and exhausted, hungry and fed up with ourselves. When we finally throw what we have grasped in our hands against the wall so that it shatters to pieces. Because only then are our hands empty again. Empty to be truly filled.*

—Fiercehearted

THIRTY-THREE

Authentic

But as for me, how good it is to be near God!
I have made the Sovereign Lord my shelter,
and I will tell everyone about the wonderful things you do.

Psalm 73:28 NLT

Just a few more minutes until you speak." These innocent words induce immediate panic. Soon I will stand in front of my entire publishing company. I have watched them file in one by one. Pressed slacks and respectable dresses. I'm the only one in jeans. I'm out of place. I'm going to fail. I bolt toward the bathroom so I can hide.

In the sudden quiet, the door locked behind me, I hear another voice—one that's still and small, audible only to me, saying, "This is not the way." God has been teaching me, so tenderly and with great patience, not to give in to fear. So I tell him what's scaring me because that's the only way to break free of its hold on my heart.

There's a knock on the door and, ready or not, it's time to go. I'm handed a mic and escorted to the front of the room. I say, "I have all the words to this speech typed out on my computer in a nice little file. I have an outline for it in my phone. I want to get everything right. I want you to approve of me. I want you to be pleased with my performance. But in reality, all I can think of is how I'm the only one in the room wearing jeans."

I talk about how Jesus is teaching me to speak what's gut-honest true. I quote this: "They triumphed over him by the blood of the Lamb and by the word of their testimony" (Rev. 12:11). Among other things, I think this means saying out loud how we're human and God is God. This calls for telling the stories where we don't show up as the prom queen in our pristine tiara, the times when we drop the spaghetti on the white shag carpet, the moments when the orange, hairy monsters are scratching our bedposts in the dark and even though we know better, we're just flat-out scared.

I used to think honoring God meant leaving all this out. But I've come to believe instead that authenticity, honesty, and having the courage to own who we are, what we live, and what we feel can mysteriously give him glory.

I think this explains why the stories and characters in Scripture seem so unedited. It's blue-sky clear that there's only one hero in God's story and it's not us. And this hero calls himself "I am who I am." I wonder if this means we, made in his image, honor him when we have the guts to say, "I am who I am" too. Even when doing so only highlights how very different we are from this beyond-our-imagination God.

There's only one hero in God's story and it's not us.

I finish speaking and there are tears in eyes. Folks come up afterward and say thank you. Women hug me. Men pound me on the back. I am clearly still the only one in the room wearing jeans. But I am clearly not the only one who has ever felt afraid or unsure or inadequate.

Sometimes we think we need to show off.

Because of Jesus, we always and only need to show up.

God, even in the moments when it seems the spotlight is on us, help us remember it's really all about you. This means we don't have to be perfect or perform, we don't have to impress or earn approval. We can simply point to you in all we say and do. Amen.

• • • • •

What's one place or way God is asking you to simply show up today? If you've felt fear or stress about that situation, take a moment to release it to him now.

What matters is that we keep showing up.

We keep releasing our vision of how we thought everything would go, how it would all unfold.

—Fiercehearted

THIRTY-FOUR

Highlight the Good

Whatever is true, whatever is noble, whatever is right, whatever is pure, whatever is lovely, whatever is admirable—if anything is excellent or praiseworthy—think about such things.

Philippians 4:8

I have a tendency to see the best in people—who they can become, the gifts they hold buried deep inside like diamonds for the mining, their potential like a seed still in the dirt and dark. Sometimes this is a blessing and a joy. But sometimes it leads to disappointment and tempts me toward disillusionment when I come to understand the current reality or when I watch someone make heartbreaking choices.

I thought perhaps I might need to give this up, to become a more reasonable sort of person who looked at folks "as is." I considered this in church the other evening in the dim light of a worship service, the shadows falling across faces. I wondered what secrets might be lurking there beneath the light, what struggles or scandals I might not know. I asked God in the quiet of my heart if I might have been fooling myself to see so much good. And this is the whisper it seemed I heard in return: "When you believe the best about people, what you believe is true. It's just not the whole story. But it's still the part worth highlighting."

I pictured the way I cradle books in my arms and pull out my highlighter—hot pink—how I run it over the lines I love most, how when I come back to that book that's what I see first. It's not that the rest of the page doesn't exist, but the highlighted parts are what I focus on before anything else.

This is the gift we can offer when we hear each other's stories. When we lay open our hearts and let the light fall on the places that have grown dusty on the shelf. We can nod our heads and say, "Oh, yes, I see what you are saying. I hear you. I acknowledge that you are imperfect because I want to give you the freedom to be so. But now I am taking out the highlighter and I'm running it across the places where you're brave and lovely, where you're making progress, where you're swinging the sword at the monster even though you're afraid it might devour you." People tend to become who we believe them to be, so let's believe the best.

People tend to become who we believe them to be, so let's believe the best.

This is the truth: when we see the best in others, we are not naïve; we are intentional. We're choosing to see what is best and letting grace cover the rest. I am committed to fighting relentlessly to keep doing so. And, yes, it means sometimes I will be disappointed. But I would rather be occasionally surprised than continually suspicious and cynical.

This is the way I hope others choose to treat me too.

When we listen to someone else's story, let's put down our swords and pick up our highlighters. Let's be safe places for the wounded to come home to, the voices in their ears and hearts reminding them of who they still are, how strong we know they can be, that we see beauty where they only see scars.

"Let the redeemed of the Lord tell their story" (Ps. 107:2). And let the redeemed of the Lord listen always and only with love and grace.

God, give us eyes of grace that see like you do. When we are tempted to complain, criticize, or condemn, remind us of how you have always loved us. Make us safe places for the hearts of others. Amen.

· · · · ·

Try to go through the next twenty-four hours without complaining about, criticizing, or condemning anyone (including yourself). Who or what makes it seem like this will be hard? Start by telling God about that situation or person here and asking for his help.

Highlight the Good

[I WANT TO SEE] NOT THE SURFACE BUT THE HEART, *not the boots but the journeyer, not the shell but the glorious, eternal being on the inside just waiting to be found and known and called worthy.*

—Fiercehearted

THIRTY-FIVE

Barefaced Beauty

The Lord does not look at the things people look at. People look at the outward appearance, but the Lord looks at the heart.

1 Samuel 16:7

My friend Suzie opens her front door and I tell her, "You look wonderful." She is naked from the neck up. When Jennifer arrives, she is as well. We are here to do another episode of *More Than Small Talk*, a video series we record in our living rooms and share online (Update: *More Than Small Talk* is now a podcast too). In a reckless conversation weeks ago, we said, "Why don't we record a video without makeup sometime? We'll call it 'Permission to Be Real.'" Maybe we would have backed out if it had been only one of us. But peer pressure is powerful, so we're here in all our non-glory.

We start our live recording and at some point in the conversation one of us asks, "What does being real mean to you?" I say that, essentially to me, it means vulnerability. It means the freedom to fully share who we are. This means that, yes, sometimes I will come without the makeup. I will show my struggles and weaknesses. I will let the tears flow. But it also means I can wear a fancy evening gown and put a tiara on my head should I choose to do so, because there are moments for this as well. Being real means being able to express the whole range of who we are, the yoga pant wearer and the wannabe princess.

We talk about how this is hard, how sometimes vulnerability is met with clichés or pat answers or misunderstanding. A phrase like "I'm struggling today" can trigger a response of "Well, you just need to trust Jesus more." When this happens, we can experience shame and guilt. But we have done nothing wrong. In that case, it's the other person who's not being real. They are hiding behind easy words and safe phrases, likely because they are afraid of life's messes, of what emotions look like close-up without mascara.

As we've already talked about, one of the greatest gifts we can offer each other when someone is real with us is to be real in return, which means offering support and a safe place for our hearts to land. It's always okay to simply say, "I hear you. I am for you. What you're going through matters to me."

It's always okay to simply say, "I hear you. I am for you. What you're going through matters to me."

Next time we do a video, Suzie, Jennifer, and I will likely have our makeup on again. I don't think being real requires letting everything about us be out there all the time. What I think it means is that we're willing to go there when God asks us to do so. We're not held back by fear or a false belief that we're only good examples when we seem perfect. God isn't looking for good examples; he's looking for imperfect people willing to make it clear why we all need a Savior.

Being real also doesn't mean defining ourselves by our worst moments and deepest struggles. This is part of our story, but it isn't all of it. David the adulterer was also David the king and warrior and poet, a man after God's own heart. This is another reason why we can be real: it doesn't change who we are. It only gives people a more complete picture of our lives, which offers them the permission to accept all of their story too. As Brené Brown says,

"We cultivate love when we allow our most vulnerable and powerful selves to be deeply seen."[1]

At the end of the video, I look at my barefaced friends and I think about how they are more beautiful than ever to me in this moment.

Love has never needed lipstick.

God, you look beyond what people see to the heart of who we are. You've seen everything about us, our bare souls, and you love us still. Help this be the true source of our confidence and security. Amen.

· · · · ·

Write 1 Samuel 16:7 on a piece of paper and place it on or near your mirror for a few days as a reminder for your heart. What thoughts come to mind when you read this verse?

Maybe we have defined beauty all wrong.

Because I have known many artists, and when a piece has what it needs to fulfill their vision for it, they stand back and say, "Beautiful." And it doesn't matter a bit to them if anyone else agrees. The artist gets the final word.

—*Fiercehearted*

THIRTY-SIX

Gentle

Be completely humble and gentle; be patient, bearing with one another in love.

Ephesians 4:2

I'm standing in front of a display of notebooks and binders in every color, a paper rainbow. Having fulfilled my obligatory shopping, I could have left the store. But I linger in the school and office supply aisle, lustfully eyeing pens and paper products. This makes me pull out the list I started only recently. I add, "I feel guilty for wasting time."

I'm writing down what makes me feel guilty because I need to see it in black-and-white rather than having it racing around in my mind like a deranged ferret, all teeth and claws and jumping. In counseling this week, I said, "Guilt is an undercurrent in my life almost all the time." My counselor, who is quite professional and helpful, looked unduly startled at this statement. I noted this because I assumed all Christians felt this—that guilt buzzed in the background of all our minds like static on an old-time radio.

I believe in grace, of course. It's not as if it doesn't play a role in my life. It's more that both guilt and grace coexist like roommates who don't speak to each other. Hence the list. I've decided I must do an inspection and force a proper interaction. I want to see what they have to say to each other and also if I ought to evict one or the other.

That evening we go to church and the sermon is about gentleness. Mark Schatzman, one of the teaching pastors, explains how we misunderstand gentleness. It is not weakness or passivity, he says—it is strength under control.[1] I scribble in the spiral-bound notebook (for eighty-eight cents, I actually felt it was a virtuous and frugal purchase, not a yield to temptation). I write this question: "What is the opposite of gentleness?" I understand in a flash: harshness. And if there is one thing that's true about the guilt voice in my mind, it's this—it is unrelentingly harsh. I realize, suddenly, that this means it can't be the voice of God or anyone representing him.

This feels scandalous and unfamiliar. I become nervous that I'm misunderstanding. But during the service we go through verse after verse about the gentleness of God. "Your gentleness makes me great" (Ps. 18:35 NASB). Jesus told us, "I am gentle and humble in heart" (Matt. 11:29 NASB). "He tends his flock like a shepherd: . . . he gently leads those that have young" (Isa. 40:11).

I'd assumed the hollering preachers and the Facebook ranters and the rule makers must be practicing righteousness. But this seems not to be the case. I write it down: I will not listen to any spiritual voice that is not speaking from a place of grace. I'm no longer going to attribute to God what is not in his heart or character. Instead, I'm going to embrace that Jesus is my advocate and defender and Savior.

Jesus is my advocate and defender and Savior.

Next time the critical voice inside me speaks, I will ask for God's help rather than hearing it as if it is from him. He is gentle. He came to set us free. He walks with us as we are. He understands our weaknesses and wandering. He has never been a God of guilt lists, only love.

God, thank you for your unfailing gentleness and kindness toward us, for the way you speak to our hearts with love and mercy. When we're tempted to think the harsh, condemning words we hear are from you, remind us of your true character. You are a God not of guilt but of grace. Amen.

• • • • •

Tune in to your thoughts today. When you hear something that brings condemnation, pause and intentionally say, "This is not from God." What is a self-critical thought you tend to have? What is the truth God wants to speak to you instead?

I'M STILL LEARNING GRACE *is not just for getting us into heaven—it is for getting us through this life.*

—Fiercehearted

THIRTY-SEVEN

Parade

Encourage each other. Live in harmony and peace. Then the God of love and peace will be with you.

2 Corinthians 13:11 NLT

I've come to a little town half an hour from mine to ride with my friend in a Christmas parade. She's representing the local Christian radio station. Whoever would like to join in the merriment is welcome. There are horses with twinkling lights wrapped around their saddles, an assortment of fire trucks, a marching band with illuminated tubas, and a man on a riding lawnmower. The theme is "The Grinch Who Stole Christmas," so a dozen or so Cindy Lou Whos are also dashing about, doing cartwheels and eating corn dogs.

When I volunteered to accompany my friend, I had not really thought through the implications, namely that a large part of being in a parade is smiling and waving wildly at strangers. My efforts are rewarded with enthusiastic responses from an assortment of parade watchers—pink-cheeked babies in the arms of their mamas, giddy toddlers with candy cane dribbles down their chins, pigtailed sweethearts wearing felt reindeer antlers.

Then we round a corner occupied by a group of moody teenage boys. Arms crossed. Heads down. Likely forced to come to the parade by evil parents. Whatever the case, one of them shouts something entirely unkind.

"What did he say?" I ask my friend. She repeats the comment. "Where is he?" I growl, beckoning her to point out the offender in the crowd. "I'm going to pummel him!" (Yes, I really used the word *pummel*. Because I am just that sophisticated and intimidating.) At this declaration her eyes grow wide. She might have hit the lock button. Thankfully, I have the sense to realize jumping out of a Christian radio station van to smack someone is not likely to result in good PR.

The moment passes and we laugh at my spontaneous response. And, of course, criticism shouldn't shock me by now. I have been alive on this earth for decades and if there's one thing I understand, it's this: yes, we have our internal critics to contend with, but there's always a critic hidden in the crowd somewhere too. Always.

Here is my rule for external critics: If you stand on the sidewalk as an uninvolved onlooker, if you are not in the parade with me, then you don't get a say. If you have not had the courage to show up, put yourself out there, open your heart, and endure the bumps in the road, then you are disqualified from giving me your opinion. Theodore Roosevelt said, "It is not the critic who counts; not the man who points out how the strong man stumbles, or where the doer of deeds could have done them better. The credit belongs to the man who is actually in the arena, whose face is marred by dust and sweat and blood . . . if he fails, at least fails while daring greatly."[1]

There are two types of folks in our worlds: the bystanders and the I'll-stand-by-you-no-matter-what kind.

There are two types of folks in our world: the bystanders and the I'll-stand-by-you-no-matter-what kind. I listen to the latter because I know if they have something hard to tell me, they are doing so from a place of love. They want what's best for me. They're praying and cheering and doing the hard work of being brave in their own lives too. They've earned the right to have a voice in my life. The critics have not.

As we make our way through our lives, the critics don't last. What remains are the faithful people like my friend in the van. And the everlasting God who came into our world because he cares for us. God isn't, as many would have us believe, the judgmental voice yelling from a distance. He is not, and never has been, the internal or external critic.

No, the scandalous secret, why the actual critics can't win, the hope that the brave, half-crazy humans need is this: on a starry night long ago, Jesus showed up in a manger and surprised the whole world by joining the parade. And he's still in it with us.

God, you understand what it is to have critics. Yours even nailed you to a cross. Yet you still love this world and reach out to the people in it. You keep your heart open. You continue to show compassion. Give us the strength to do the same. Amen.

· · · · ·

Who in your life is facing criticism, perhaps from a boss, a teenage son or daughter, or even their own heart? Write their name here and offer that person a word of encouragement in some way today.

....

....

....

....

....

We're stronger than we know,

braver than we think, and the universe needs true, audacious kindness more than ever.

—Fiercehearted

THIRTY-EIGHT

Vulnerable

But you are a chosen people, a royal priesthood, a holy nation, God's special possession, that you may declare the praises of him who called you out of darkness into his wonderful light.

1 Peter 2:9

On an ordinary afternoon, I curled up on my red couch, my phone tucked between my ear and shoulder. I nodded as I listened to my friend far away share about a challenge in her life. At some point she said, "I guess this is who I am now. I am the girl who struggles with this thing."

I sat up straight, grabbed my phone so I could speak as loudly and directly into it as I could, and the nodding ceased. I said, "No, that is not who you are now. That is not who you are ever. This is your current circumstance. It is what you are fighting. It is not and will never be your identity." Long after our call was over, I kept thinking about those words. Yes, they came from my mouth, but I knew they also came from God's heart. They were important for my friend to hear, but they were also important for me to say because they caused a permanent shift in my perspective.

I thought of that moment again recently when I spoke at a retreat in another country and shared my story. I spoke of my fears and insecurities, failures and shortcomings, the battles I've fought and the scars I have to prove it. I watched the tissues pulled out of pockets and the head nods. After the event, women kept pulling me aside. They'd tug on my arm or beckon me with a head tilt gesturing toward a quiet corner of the room. In all these conversations, the same question was asked: "How can you be so vulnerable?"

The question surprised me because I hadn't considered it until then. At first I didn't know how to answer. But slowly, finally, I said, "I can be vulnerable because my struggles are part of my circumstances, not my identity. I'm not my successes. I'm not my failures. I'm a beloved daughter of God."

I'm not my successes. I'm not my failures. I'm a beloved daughter of God.

On the outside this sounds simple, like it could be put in a Sunday school diagram with arrows and lines. Yet the reality is often full of messes and heartache and so many undoings. Keeping hold of who we are is like wrestling a wild alligator most days. I suppose this will always be so, that it is the way of being human in this world. Vulnerability and security and showing up as we are do not come easy. But, I am finding, they are worth the fight.

The enemy of our hearts would love to convince us that we are our struggles or our failures, our mistakes or our secrets. If we let this happen, then shame wins and we hide. But we are never, ever defined by what we do. We are always and only defined by what Jesus has done for us. Because of his death on the cross and his resurrection from the grave, sin has been defeated, death has been overcome, and even the darkest moments of our lives can't diminish his light within us.

Let's never stop shining. Let's never stop speaking of what he has done for us. Let's never believe our circumstances are more powerful than the grace of our Savior.

God, thank you for what you did for us on the cross and through the resurrection. In the moments when it's tempting to believe what we've done or what has been done to us is our identity, remind us that you created us and saved us, and only you get to say who we are. Amen.

• • • • •

How have you defined who you are? Think of how you'd fill in this blank: I am ____________________. Is there anything that contradicts what God says about you? If so, release it now and replace it with truth.

SOMEWHERE A SNAKE HISSES *and a Savior on a cross declares, "It is finished." A single red drop falls to the ground. The curtain splits and the curse breaks and the promise of Eden comes back to us. All the sisters and the daughters and the mamas say, "Amen."*

—Fiercehearted

THIRTY-NINE

Freedom Giver

Love does not delight in evil but rejoices with the truth.

1 Corinthians 13:6

I'm escorted to a pretend kitchen with pale blue cabinets and bright lights overhead. A mic is run awkwardly down my dress. I sit in front of a coffee mug that actually has water instead of coffee in it (sad). Melinda, the host of *See, Hear, Love* and the rest of the women on this Christian Canadian talk show take their places beside me. My heart beats like a rock-and-roll drummer and I wonder, suddenly, if I have something in my nose. But it's too late—the camera has begun to roll.

I can't recall everything I say. I know the ladies ask questions and I answer. We laugh and bare our hearts as if no one's watching. But for the rest of my days, I will remember one response I gave. Because until that very moment it had never, ever occurred to me. I was asked about the power of telling our struggles. And I said, "Jesus told us, 'The truth will set you free,' and, yes, I believe this applies first and foremost to the gospel. But I think it also means that when we speak the truth of our struggles and stories, we help set each other free too."

This idea feels entirely new to me in that moment. And yet haven't I lived it? Haven't we all? I picture being across from a friend and clearing my throat, finally putting words to the darkness I've been battling. I think of the freedom that comes when she says, "Me too." I imagine coming across sentences in a book that put words to something I thought no one else had ever faced and the shock and joy of "I'm not the only one" breaking the chains around my heart. I think of my friend Christy again, the one sitting on the black stool telling her story, and how the courage of her speaking the truth of her life that night loosened us all up inside.

When we speak the truth of our struggles and stories, we help set each other free.

I also remember moments when I've bit my tongue, when I've smiled and said the polite words, how I felt tangled up in my soul. I can recall holding back, holding it all in, and how silence seemed like a prison.

I'm not advocating that we go around sharing all things with all people. That would be both unwise and downright dangerous. What I'm saying is that there is a time and a place and a people with whom speaking truth can bring true freedom.

The show continues. The interview is about *Fiercehearted*, and at the end we talk about remembering we're warriors. We close by roaring together. The woman next to me is like a lioness, loud and clear and brave. And I'm like a kitten, with a mew that wouldn't scare a housefly. The camera is turned off, but the impact of that new truth on my life still goes on to this day, to this very moment.

I want to be a woman who speaks the truth of her story. I want to be a woman who brings God glory. I want to be a woman who helps set her sisters free.

God, you are the truth, and when we speak what's true, we align with who you are, with how we're created to live. Give us the courage we need to speak our story and the wisdom to know when it's time to be silent too. Thank you for setting our hearts free. Amen.

.....

We're asked so often, "How are you?" and it's easy to quickly say, "I'm fine." If someone you trust to listen well asks you that today and you have more to say, then consider sharing in a deeper way. Write what you would say here as practice.

It's in the telling,

in the opening, that we begin to see our stories for what they are—glory-filled and flawed works of art. We start giving (and, yes, getting) what all our tattered-cover lives really need. Not comparison. A little more compassion.

—*Fiercehearted*

FORTY

Dark, Light

The light shines in the darkness, and the darkness has not overcome it.

John 1:5

I don't feel strong or brave this morning. My alarm woke me at 4 a.m., long before sunrise. The sky outside was still thick black. I tried to burrow under the covers for a few more moments while my husband headed for the shower. He's having minor surgery today and we had to show up for pre-op as soon as the clinic opened. I've been battling a cold that has very clearly and suddenly turned into a sinus infection. I hit a bird with my car on the way to the clinic. The waiting room Wi-Fi isn't working. I just want to go back to bed.

I'm writing in the middle of all this because you will have moments like this as well. It is part of being on this earth. We don't have to like these moments. We are allowed to feel tired and frustrated and sad. But they are inevitable.

As we drove to the clinic, I noticed a few stars scattered across the sky. The last time I was up this early I found myself in an entirely different kind of setting, a totally different sort of moment. Mark and I were on vacation at the beach and we'd gotten up early to watch the sunrise. I noted the stars then, too, and one star in particular caught my attention. I found out later it was actually the planet Venus, otherwise known as the Morning Star. Here is its mystery and beauty: Venus is known for rising in the darkest part of the night. Jesus said, "I am the . . . bright Morning Star" (Rev. 22:16). I think this means, among other things, he is not afraid of the deepest dark. He is not frightened by the hard moments of our lives. He is not afraid to step right into the worst of it with us. It also means that the darkness will not last forever. The light will come again.

When Mark and I walked through the clinic door this morning, I realized I'd been here years ago when he had a procedure for a torn ligament in his knee. My breath caught in my throat for a moment. "The last time I was here I was pregnant," I told him. A few days later I would miscarry. That felt like the darkest night, as if light would never come. But as you know by now, that wasn't the end. Our decade of infertility gave way to a daughter and then a granddaughter. Sometimes the light feels so bright now my heart can hardly take it all in. It's like looking right at the sun.

Courage means standing in the dark and still believing the light will come.

This is what I'm leaning on this morning, what we can cling to always: We don't have to feel strong or brave; we only need to never give up hope. Courage means standing in the dark and still believing the light will come. We are not done. God isn't either.

PS: Mark made it through surgery just fine.

God, you are the light of the world and no darkness can overcome you, which means no darkness can overcome us. In the moments when it feels like the night of our hearts will last forever, give us hope that a new day is coming. Amen.

. . . . .

Dark, Light

Watch the sunrise or look at the evening stars today as a reminder that the darkness cannot overcome the light. What darkness are you battling? How can you see God bringing light into it?

WHATEVER HAPPENS, GOD IS WITH US AND FOR US. *Whatever obstacles we encounter, we can overcome them. Whatever this world may do, we're going to keep being courageous.*

—Fiercehearted

FORTY-ONE

Waters Recede

Be still in the presence of the Lord,
and wait patiently for him to act.
Psalm 37:7 NLT

Our house is quiet when I climb the stairs to my little office. It has been a long day and I sit cross-legged on the carpet like a kindergartener. I tell God all the things on my mind—the worries and fears, questions and concerns. I don't pray eloquently. My words are messy and scattered. What comes out of my mouth sounds entirely unspiritual to me. I don't know how to do it any differently.

When I'm done, I stand at the window and look out over a gray afternoon. Then I see it in the distance—a rainbow. I turn to my trusty whiteboard and I write something new. Three simple words: *write, pray, wait*. As soon as I do, it feels like my heart sighs in relief.

I think then of Noah after the flood when the first rainbow appeared. Surely as soon as the last drop of rain fell, he was ready to get off that boat. But it took time for the waters to recede. So he stayed where God had placed him. He prayed. He waited. Then, finally, the time was right to leave the ark, to embrace what God had next for him.

When we've had a flood in our lives—a significant change or a loss or even a new opportunity that threatens to overwhelm us—it can be tempting to want to get back to "normal" as quickly as possible. That's what I wanted when I went upstairs to pray. I wanted God to fix everything right then and there. But, I'm finding, the waters take time to recede in our lives too. And even when they do, things never go back to the way they were before. We learn a new normal, a different way of being. It takes courage to embrace this. It takes guts to be patient as everything unfolds. Sometimes the bravest move is to stay where you are and simply see what God will do.

Sometimes the bravest move is to stay where you are and simply see what God will do.

I want to share this because when we are in a season when we're waiting for the waters to recede in our lives, we can feel stuck or discouraged. We can believe we must be missing God's will for us. We can get hard on ourselves because it all feels so slow.

But our ways are not like God's, our timing is not like his. He is working out his eternal plan, and he understands the importance of the pause we're in right now. He could have made the waters recede instantly for Noah. But he didn't. Why? I have no idea. And we will likely have no clue why he takes so much time with particular challenges in our lives too.

What we can know is that we are where we're supposed to be right now. We will not be there a moment longer than we're intended to be. But we will not be released a moment sooner either. We can rest in knowing that today. We can keep serving wherever we've been placed in this season. We can wait. We can pray.

God, your timing and ways are so different from ours. Give us the wisdom to know when to move forward and when to simply be still and wait for you. We trust you to guide us every moment. Amen.

. . . . .

Write Psalm 37:7 on a sticky note and place it on a clock in your home as a reminder for your heart this week. What thoughts does this verse bring to mind for you?

PERHAPS, IN THE END, SHARING ALL OF LIFE *with God is what praying really means. It's that line, "Thy kingdom come, Thy will be done" [Matt. 6:10 KJV]. It's not about getting what we want or proving something to God. Instead, it's about aligning our hearts with his. It's about heaven-come-here.*

—Fiercehearted

FORTY-TWO

Rest, Trust, Repeat

Wait patiently for the Lord.
Be brave and courageous.
Yes, wait patiently for the Lord.
Psalm 27:14 NLT

I am a completer by nature. Give me a checklist or a project or dishes to put away. I will roll up my sleeves, invite the sweat, and smile with satisfaction. So when Jesus declares, "I have brought you glory on earth by finishing the work you gave me to do" (John 17:4), I am interested.

I am ready to be busy. I want to perform well. I will hustle in the name of holiness. This makes me feel safe.

See me nodding with the dusty-footed crowd when they ask Jesus, "We want to perform God's works, too. What should we do?" (John 6:28 NLT). I am pulling out my newly sharpened pencil, ready to take notes. Then comes the reply: "The work of God is this: to believe in the one he has sent" (John 6:29).

I pause, unsure hand hovering over the page, and tilt my head in confusion. Did I hear that right? He only wants me to believe? I should be relieved. Instead, I feel inexplicably disappointed. Because if that's it, if that's all, then it's not about me. And it's sure not about being perfect.

Hayley Morgan says in *Wild and Free*, "The opposite of faith isn't doubt, it's control."[1] These words reach all the way down to my self-strong and stubborn bones.

Because the reality is, I feel safer when I'm working hard for God. It's easier to tell myself I am worthy when I am in the midst of proving it. Strip me of my spiritual stunts and I am an awkward performer on a stage, hoping for what? Applause for simply being there?

But the applause was never intended for us anyway and the spotlight is always and only to be swung away from us and toward God. Our work is simply to bear witness to his Word made flesh and to say a yes and an amen to him with all our lives.

Jesus loves us, this I know, for the Bible tells me so.

This is the truest theology. This is the hum and rhythm our souls are made to dance to. We are not workers, after all; *we are worshipers*. We are the broken made whole, the fallen and rescued, the messy and undeserving children jumping in endless puddles of rained-down grace.

Jesus loves us, this I know, for the Bible tells me so.

God, give us the courage to live as beloved believers today. The ones whose souls have no hard-work calluses. The trusters who trade our pencils for an old wooden cross. The unexpectedly brave who look at the spinning, striving world and dare to say, "God is good. We are loved. That is all."

God, thank you for calling us to a life not of doing but of being. Of choosing love. Of receiving grace. Of resting in you. In a hurry-hurry, try-hard world, this is brave. We choose to trust in you. Amen.

• • • • •

Try creating a not-to-do list for today with at least three items on it.

Today I will not . . .

DON'T LET ANYONE TRICK YOU *into believing what you're on earth to do can easily be printed on a business card or typed in neat lines on a résumé. You are on this earth to be—which is really just another way of saying you're here to love and be loved.*

—Fiercehearted

FORTY-THREE

Always Coming

I will not leave you as orphans; I will come to you.

John 14:18

My daughter and I sit on the couch in my living room and read the familiar story. The Garden of Eden. Eve. The forbidden fruit. The fall. We are going through a series of passages called "From Creation to Christ" and, of course, this scene makes the list. It's where everything changes, after all.

Afterward we walk around the neighborhood on a blue-sky summer day and talk about what we've read. What does this tell us about God? What does this tell us about people? How does this change how we live? Three simple, complicated questions.

Before I know it, I'm saying this: "God always comes for us. He came for Adam and Eve when they were hiding in shame. He came for his people when they were enslaved in Egypt. He came to Bethlehem. He's coming again."

Perhaps I've known this always but sometimes a truth shines out at you in a new way like a bit of gold in the mining pan. I look over at my daughter and recall how just a few days ago she called and said, "I just need a hug." And I came. Of course I did. I told her, "That's what mamas are for."

I think then of how it's hard sometimes for me to believe God does the same for me in the messy, ordinary, everyday moments of life. I act instead like I have to find a way to be good enough to come to him. If I try harder, do more, read my Bible, hold my tongue, be a good girl, then maybe I can dare to enter into his presence.

But God scandalously doesn't wait for us to get it together. He comes right into the Garden while the fruit is still half eaten on the ground. He finds us where we are hiding in fear and wrestling with regret. He comes to the places where we feel trapped, where it seems no matter how much we want change, we just can't be free. He comes to the humble and mundane—not to the fancy, prepared inn but to the manger, to the places we deem far too improper and unlovely for him. He will come for us today and tomorrow and on our final day when we take our last breath.

Why? Because that's what Love does. He comes when we are unworthy. He comes when we are overwhelmed. He comes when we are weary. He comes when we are insecure. He comes when we are doubting. He comes when we are broken. He comes when we just need a hug.

We do not need to earn our way to God. We only need to open our hearts and see that he is already here with us and he's told us, "I will never leave you or abandon you" (Heb. 13:5 CSB).

Love will always come for us.

This is the truth all our hearts need to know today: Love came for us. Love will always come for us. And, no matter what, he's not leaving.

God, thank you for always coming for us, even when we don't deserve it and although we could never earn it. We are so grateful for your faithful love. Your presence in our lives helps us be strong, brave, and loved. Amen.

• • • • •

God shows his presence with us in many ways.
What's one way you've seen his love in your life lately?

THIS IS ALL I'M SURE *is true of all of me: every part of who I am needs Jesus more than I even fully understand, more than I can really find the right words to say.*

—Fiercehearted

FORTY-FOUR

World-Changer

And if anyone gives even a cup of cold water to one of these little ones who is my disciple, truly I tell you, that person will certainly not lose their reward.

Matthew 10:42

I'm part of a panel at a women's event, and when it's my turn to hold the microphone, I suddenly feel sweaty. My heart pounds like I've had a double espresso. I'm asked this question: "Do you consider yourself to be a world-changer?" I'm caught off guard for a moment, blinded by the spotlight above me and all the eyes on me. When I gather my wits about me again, I say, "My sweet daddy once told me that every day he prays my words will touch the heart of one woman who will touch the heart of her family who will touch the hearts of their community who will touch the world. So, yes, in that way I consider myself to be a world-changer."

I believe being a world-changer simply means touching the heart of one person at a time through whatever gifts we've been given right where we are today. That one person for you might be a friend, a coworker, someone in your family, or a stranger on the street. Your gift might be words or encouraging, organizing or baking, leading or creating spreadsheets.

It doesn't matter if the couch we're sitting on is on a stage or in a living room. We can be equally impactful holding a microphone or heating mac and cheese in the microwave for the people we love. We can make a difference from a downtown office or the driver's seat of a minivan.

Yes, what I do has its "spotlight" moments. But as I've said before, most of my work is done alone in front of a keyboard in yoga pants. It can sometimes feel hard and lonely. It can sometimes seem like there's no one on the other side of the screen. It can be tempting to believe what I do doesn't matter because I don't have anything tangible to show for it at the end of the day.

This is the lie the enemy would like us to believe: Only certain people are world-changers. The kind who seem to do big, extraordinary things. God alone is big and extraordinary. He uses small, ordinary people to change the world every day because that's the only kind there are, the only kind there will ever be. That includes you and me.

> Being a world-changer simply means touching the heart of one person at a time through whatever gifts we've been given right where we are today.

Zechariah 4:10 says, "The people should not think that small beginnings are unimportant" (ICB). The people should not think small middles or endings are unimportant either. All the moments of our lives can be meaningful when they are in the hands of an almighty God. Have faith the size of a mustard seed, Jesus said, and you'll move mountains (Matt. 17:20).

So if, like me, you've ever wondered if what you're doing matters, if you've been unsure you're making a difference, if you've been tempted to compare, then let's pause together and realign our perspectives with God's heart. He has placed us here for such a time as this and he is working in and through us in ways beyond what we can see. What seems like nothing at all in this moment might just change all of eternity.

God, thank you for giving meaning to every moment of our lives, whether they seem big or small in the eyes of the world. Help us remember that it's not the size of what we do but the size of the God we serve that matters. We will serve you in the spotlight. We will serve you when no one sees. We love you. Amen.

· · · · ·

What's one small, perhaps even invisible, way you can love God and others today?

No pedestals present.

Only ordinary, feet-on-the-ground folks figuring life out together. Maybe humble, holy ground is the only vantage point where we can really see each other, where we just might proceed to change the world.

—*Fiercehearted*

FORTY-FIVE

Holy Confidence

Bring . . . my daughters from the ends of the earth—
everyone who is called by my name,
whom I created for my glory,
whom I formed and made.

Isaiah 43:6–7

I had a home perm in third grade. Those of you who lived through that era know what I'm talking about, and those of you who didn't should be glad you missed it. My well-intentioned grandma and mama sat me down in a chair right in the middle of the kitchen. I can still smell the chemicals worthy of an environmental cleanup crew. I can feel the slight burn of who knows what transforming my straight hair into the lovely tendrils portrayed on the home perm box. Needless to say, the outcome did not quite match the optimistic hopes of my relatives. When we look back at pictures of me in third grade, my family still says, "So adorable!" and I still ask, "Were you trying to ruin my life?"

It's around this age that we start being told that the secret to all our troubles is to have more self-esteem. The home perm did nothing for me in this area. Neither did the mantras I was told to repeat. The ones like "I'm smart enough,

I'm good enough, and people like me." They rang hollow even then and they still don't do much for me now.

I thought of all this when someone recently asked me, "Do you ever struggle with self-esteem? It looks like you have it all together." I've been asked this before, told this before, and it still surprises and startles me. Because I can see my insides. I know my messes and my crazy, my mistakes and my stumbles, how I've wrestled with depression and anxiety like wild alligators, how my heart has the scars to prove it. I've also been witness to the home perm pictures.

What I've been realizing lately, and what I said in answer to that question, is this: *the world tells us we need to have self-esteem, but what we really need is holy confidence.* For years I tried to prove I was enough. Perfect enough. Good enough. Experienced enough. Smart enough. Pretty enough. But it's only when we come to the place where we can finally say, "I'm not enough but Jesus is" that our hearts get free.

The reality is we will always fall short of the expectations of others and ourselves. We will always have some version of the home perm going on in our lives. But it doesn't matter, because our scandalous God, our gracious Savior, declares we are beloved and chosen and empowered *anyway*.

Self-esteem says we can do it.

Holy confidence says, in spite of us, God will.

Self-esteem says we can belong in the right crowd.

Holy confidence says we belong to the Creator of the universe.

Self-esteem says our worth comes from what's external.

Holy confidence says our worth comes from what's eternal.

Self-esteem says we can do it. Holy confidence says, in spite of us, God will.

We are daughters of God created in his image. We are chosen to be part of his plan. We are promised that we will have everything we need for all he has called us to do. We have been forgiven and set free. This is the source of our hope. This is our security. This is why, in spite of our weaknesses and failures (and even home perms), we can walk in holy confidence today.

God, you are the One who determines our worth. You offer us so much more than self-esteem; you give us holy confidence. Help us embrace that and walk boldly in it no matter what the world around us may say. Amen.

• • • • •

As you watch commercials, take part in conversations, or even scroll through social media, listen for messages telling you who you're supposed to be. If those messages don't align with what God says about you, pause and say to your own heart, "I don't have to believe that's true." What is one of those messages you've been tempted to believe? What does God say instead?

WE ARE WORKS OF ART *who can say to God, "You knit me together in my mother's womb" (Ps. 139:13).*

—Fiercehearted

FORTY-SIX

Only the Lonely

Each heart knows its own bitterness,
and no one else can fully share its joy.
Proverbs 14:10 NLT

I'm sitting on the balcony of a hotel at a table of women whose names you probably know, whose faces you'd likely recognize. In between sips of coffee, we start to share our secrets. We all have this one in common: sometimes we feel lonely.

Loneliness is a hard thing to talk about in this era of friending and liking and sharing with the entire universe. To admit to even a moment of loneliness feels like dropping a shield and standing barehearted on the battlefield. But maybe what we think is a shield is actually a wall, and hiding behind it actually makes us more alone. Maybe it's time to tear down that wall.

I want to start by saying that there's no shame in being lonely sometimes. I think we get confused about this a lot. We think lonely means we are standing by ourselves on the playground after everyone has been picked for the team. We think lonely means there must be something wrong with us. We think lonely is the purple stain on our white dress that will make everyone stare.

But lonely is simply this: a symptom of being human. "Each heart knows its own bitterness, and no one else can fully share its joy" (Prov. 14:10 NLT). This explains why we can feel all by ourselves in a crowd. Why sometimes when we're sitting on the floor in our pajamas on Christmas morning with everyone we love around, we still feel an odd longing. Why we turn nineteen and wistful all over again when we hear that old love song come over the loudspeakers in the store.

But lonely is simply this: a symptom of being human.

Loneliness is really a desire to be completely connected to someone else. And, in this world, that's simply not possible. Yes, there are friendships made at summer camp and in boardrooms. There are marriages that last over half a century. There are sisters we are born to and those of our own making. But even then, even those, don't mean that sometimes we won't feel lonely. I say this not to be discouraging but to help us stop taking loneliness personally.

I think loneliness tells us better than perhaps anything else what we really want from community. If I'm always lonely in groups, then I am probably craving one-on-one time, a meaningful conversation over coffee. If I always leave the coffee shop feeling disconnected, then perhaps what I really need is to play and have fun with a lively tribe. Loneliness also makes us appreciate the people we do have in our lives. And loneliness draws us closer to Jesus, the One who knows us completely and fully.

When we see the folks whose lives seem to be an endless party full of people, we can say, "It's not their turn for loneliness right now. But it has been before and it will be again." We can also remember that what we perceive is not necessarily the reality. Years ago a well-known author and speaker said to me, "The wider my message gets, the lonelier I feel." I've never forgotten those words.

That morning on the balcony I realized loneliness doesn't have to be a secret we keep from each other. Instead, it's something we all have in common that can bring us together. We all live with these two truths: Yes, sometimes we are lonely. Yes, we are always loved.

God, you lived in this world and faced everything we do. It seems that would include moments of loneliness too. When we feel alone, remind us you are with us and comfort our hearts. Give us eyes that notice others who may be lonely, too, and show us how we can come alongside them. Amen.

· · · · ·

Who in your life might be lonely today?
What's a small way you can let them know they're not alone?

....

....

....

....

....

....

....

WHEN YOU GET TO THE END *of these pages, I want you to also be able to say with certainty, "I'm not the only one."*

—Fiercehearted

FORTY-SEVEN

Incomparable

Make a careful exploration of who you are and the work you have been given, and then sink yourself into that. Don't be impressed with yourself. Don't compare yourself with others. Each of you must take responsibility for doing the creative best you can with your own life.

Galatians 6:4–5 MSG

One sticky summer in college, I lived in a run-down motel in a room the color of mangos. I wrote about this in *Fiercehearted*, about how a bright green hose stuck out of the shower wall like a misplaced vine. How I had two roommates and fifty-eight more housemates, all of us crammed together, with girls upstairs and boys down, sharing three months of work and life and ministry.

Summer has just turned up the thermostat here and I'm thinking of that time again. How on the first day, we stood circled in the living room and all I could focus on was how my shorts stuck to my thighs in the unair-conditioned living room. *Her* shorts didn't seem to be climbing her leg like an impetuous toddler. *Her* voice didn't seem so quiet when asked the simplest questions, like "What's your name? Where are you from?" *Her* purple plaid bedspread didn't seem so faded and plain.

Compare. Compare. Compare.

I'd showed up, but I wasn't really there.

I wish I could say this was the first time comparison stole from me, snatched my joy or time or presence of mind. But we both know it's not. It's also not the last. Because I'm a daughter of Eve, descended from the woman in Eden who heard a serpent hissing lies, the implication being "You are not enough" and "God is holding out on you."

The lies of comparison still hiss at my heart, especially through social media. It's so easy to make an "ideal life" collage in our minds with her vacation and someone else's cute kids, that woman's dream job and this one's red brick house in the suburbs. But it's fantasy, because it's the highlight reel of fifty different people. Meanwhile, the perfect kids are throwing spaghetti at the ceiling and they all got the stomach flu on the cruise and the contractor just told them about the crack in the foundation.

This is what's real and true: We have strengths, skills, and gifts no one else does. God has a mission for our lives only we can fulfill. There never has been and never will be another us. And when there is only one of something, it simply can't be compared. Our Maker gets to choose who we are. He gets to decide which doors open for us and which ones stay closed. He is the Creator and the Savior and the One who looks at us and calls us beloved.

> God doesn't want us to be more like anyone but Jesus.

This is the truth I'm learning, the one I wish I could go back and whisper to my nineteen-year-old self as I stood in the living room of that run-down hotel, the one I'm declaring to all of us now: God doesn't want us to be more like anyone but Jesus.

God, you created us to be who we are, and you don't compare us to anyone else. Whew, that's so reassuring to know. When we are tempted to compare, remind us of who you've made us and how much we're already loved. Then show us how we can help others be who you've designed them to be too. Amen.

· · · · ·

If you could go back to your nineteen-year-old self, what would you say to her today?

I THOUGHT IF I COULD JUST *be successful enough, I would become someone else. But you can't grow into someone new. You can only grow into more of you.*

—Fiercehearted

FORTY-EIGHT

Heart Gate

Above all else, guard your heart,
for everything you do flows from it.
Proverbs 4:23

We are sitting in a living room with robin's-egg blue walls—a lovely fragile color—and clean white trim. My friend asks a question tentatively, as if throwing a pebble at a window. She doesn't want to break anything. She just needs to release this question into the universe: "What if allowing yourself to be loved means someone may hurt you?"

This is a brave woman who serves and speaks and writes. I pause for a moment, feeling the weight of this question. We have been talking about how and why letting love in can be so hard. About how it seems we can all be in the business of constructing walls that seem like they will keep us safe. We know how to build barriers. But, really, this is not what any of us want.

I say slowly as it comes to me like the slow light of sun over the horizon, "I think what makes a difference is making sure we have a gate in the wall." We don't shut ourselves completely off, but we don't leave ourselves wide open either. This is the paradox of what it means to "above all else, guard your heart" (Prov. 4:23) and at the same time follow the example of a Savior who stretched wide on a cross.

Even if we have a gate in our hearts, we can sometimes lock it in two ways. First, we can do so from the inside, through perfectionism or people-pleasing, legalism or trying so very hard. We turn the key, hear the click that means no one is getting too close, and tell ourselves we'll open ourselves up again only when we are finally worthy and perfect.

Or we bar the gate from the outside because we've grown weary of all the broken people in this world who scratch our souls with their sharp edges. We retreat to where it is pristine and safe, where nothing and no one can touch us. Then we wonder why we feel all alone. It's learning to live without these inner and outer defenses that is so hard. But, because of Jesus, it is not impossible.

If I had a security screener, like the ones at the airport, it would look like 1 Corinthians 13:4–7. "Love is patient, love is kind. It does not envy, it does not boast, it is not proud. It does not dishonor others, it is not self-seeking, it is not easily angered, it keeps no record of wrongs. Love does not delight in evil but rejoices with the truth. It always protects, always trusts, always hopes, always perseveres."

When we are deciding whether or not to open the gate to someone, we can use love to evaluate. We can ask, "What is the pattern of this person's life?" If the answer aligns with 1 Corinthians 13, then it's likely safe to let them through. But if the pattern sets off the alarms, then it's okay to be cautious. This doesn't mean we don't love that person; it simply means we don't have to give them an all-access pass to our heart.

Here's a check for us too: *Are we safe for others?* Yes, even the relationships we value most will sometimes have disagreements and misunderstandings. But overall, the pattern is to be love as God defines it.

If our gate is locked from the inside, let's dare to allow ourselves to be loved as we are. If it's barred from the outside, let's ask God about the next step in the healing process. And no matter what happens, let's remember that God loves us and wants to be with us where we are, as we are, today. He will give us the courage and wisdom to guard our hearts. We are worth protecting.

God loves us and wants to be with us where we are, as we are, today.

God, you understand how hard it is to love sometimes and how fragile our hearts can be. We ask for wisdom to know how to love others with both compassion and discernment. Give us the courage and wisdom to guard our hearts. Amen.

• • • • •

Take a moment to think about the "gate" of your heart today. What's one way you can open it? What's one circumstance or relationship in which closing it would be appropriate?

I sensed Jesus—

very kind and tender and knowing far more than I what it is to feel crucified, waiting quietly for me to decide what to do.

—*Fiercehearted*

FORTY-NINE

Awkward

We belong to each other, and each needs all the others.

Romans 12:5 TLB

I've had a week filled with awkward. It still happens.

First, I went to a women's event where I hardly knew anyone. I stood in the foyer picking at a plate of pasta while my heart almost pounded out of my chest. I attempted to make small talk. I went to the bathroom three times in forty-five minutes just to hide. I occasionally stared at my phone so it would seem like someone, somewhere, might know and like me.

Now here's the thing: last fall I did a speaking event at this very same place. I stood on the stage and talked about being fiercehearted with calmness and confidence. I signed books and snapped pictures with a couple hundred folks. But this casual mingling in the foyer was so much harder.

A couple of evenings later, I sat around a table with a group of local writers. As we talked about books and blog posts and what it's like to be in the world of words, I felt the same anxiety coming back. My cheeks felt hot, my shirt got sticky with sweat, and my inner critic became so loud I could hardly hear anything else. I had known many of these women online before I met them in real life, and connecting with them only online made me feel safe because I could hide the parts of me I didn't want them to see. I could be confident and witty. I never said "um" or laughed at the wrong time or worried about my hair.

My husband and I are hooked on the television show *Nashville* right now (don't judge), and one of the main characters, singer Juliette Barnes, said something that keeps ringing in my ears. Her personal life is a train wreck, but as she's about to step on stage to do a concert, she remarks, "Oh, it's easy to make twenty thousand people love you."[1]

Isn't that what our world tells us? Post the perfect pictures on Instagram. Work the crowd. Craft an image. Create an audience instead of meaningful relationships. Avoid all the awkward.

But despite its difficulties, I'm falling in love with the awkward. It's where we find out which one of our friends laughs so hard she snorts. It's where the mascara runs right down our faces and we discover how lovely the ugly cry can be. It's where we remember we are not God—and that is a very good thing. It's where we learn to believe we're loved for who we are and not who we sometimes wish we could be.

By the end of the women's ministry event, I'd found someone to sit with and made a new friend. When the writer get-together was over, I stood in the parking lot talking with two of the women about God and our own hearts as the summer sky turned indigo blue. I'm so glad I didn't miss those moments.

Awkward is the price of admission for authentic connection. It costs us; oh, how it does. It costs our pride and our desire to be seen as perfect and the comfort of our couches. I hope I'm always willing to pay it.

Awkward is the price of admission for authentic connection.

The people who impress me most these days are not the ones on stages or those with the most likes on their social media pages. I'm impressed with the folks who show up in the everyday and say, "Here I am. There you are.

Let's figure out how to love each other." That is a brave, beautiful, world-changing thing.

And I think this kind of living is what Jesus shows us. He came not to a throne but to a manger. He sought a cross, not a spotlight. He didn't stay at a distance but instead walked the dusty, messy roads with us. In other words, he could have made twenty thousand people love him, but instead he pursued hearts one by one. He still does.

May he give us the courage to do the same.

God, thank you for pursuing our hearts, for coming to this earth, for living right in the middle of all our awkward. When fear tempts us to hold back from connecting, give us the courage to show up as we are and love like you do. Amen.

• • • • •

When do you feel awkward? What helps give you the courage to push through that feeling and connect anyway?

But I don't believe this battle

is only about me. It's about all my sisters. It's about all my daughters. It's about every woman in this world. Because every time one of us wins, we all do. We silence the roar of darkness a little more.

—*Fiercehearted*

FIFTY

Barista

He knows how weak we are;
he remembers we are only dust.
Psalm 103:14 NLT

Every few months I want to quit everything and become a barista in Australia. The people I'm closest to know this about me. So when I sat down next to a friend yesterday and declared this to her, she didn't even flinch. She just grinned, shoved a cup of coffee and half a muffin toward me, and told me to pull out my computer and start typing.

Here's the thing: we're all going to want to quit sometimes. We're all going to get fed up and worn out. We expect this when life is hard, but what we need to know, what I want to talk about now, is how this also happens when we're experiencing a new level of victory in our lives. I call this "The Elijah Effect" because I first learned about it from an Old Testament prophet who did his own version of wanting to move to Australia and become a barista.

Elijah challenged four hundred prophets of the false god Baal to a showdown. He would build an altar to his God. They would build one for Baal. Whichever god sent down fire to consume the offering would be declared the true one. Of course, Elijah's God showed up and showed off. Elijah prayed and "immediately the fire of the LORD flashed down from heaven. . . . And when all the people saw it, they fell face down on the ground and cried out, 'The LORD—he is God! Yes, the LORD is God!'" (1 Kings 18:38–39 NLT).

After this victory you'd expect that Elijah was on a spiritual high, more filled with faith than ever. Instead, "He went on alone into the wilderness, traveling all day. He sat down under a solitary broom tree and prayed that he might die. 'I have had enough, LORD,' he said. 'Take my life, for I am no better than my ancestors who have already died'" (1 Kings 19:4 NLT). Then Elijah fell asleep.

I love this scene because it's so ridiculously human. I love that God included it in Scripture. I love even more that God didn't rebuke Elijah. He let him nap, then sent an angel with divine room service and this deeply spiritual message: "Get up and eat" (1 Kings 19:7 NLT).

Victory in our lives is wonderful and exhilarating. Having God use us in powerful ways is thrilling. It's also flat-out exhausting. When we don't acknowledge this, we start declaring we're moving to Australia or wind up sitting under a tree in the middle of nowhere asking God to take us on home. In those moments, we can show the same kind of compassion to ourselves that God does to us. And sometimes the godliest thing we can do is take a nap and have a snack.

> In our highest highs and lowest lows, God and those around us remember we are human. We're wise to do the same.

I finished my coffee, half a muffin, and a blog post (writing renews my soul). Then I told my friend I was not going to Australia after all. For some reason, she didn't look surprised. Elijah "got up and ate and drank, and the food gave him enough strength to travel forty days and forty nights to Mount Sinai, the mountain of God" (1 Kings 19:8 NLT). His meltdown in the wilderness didn't disqualify him from the next victory.

Here's what I'm learning: in our highest highs and lowest lows, God and those around us remember we are human. We're wise to do the same.

God, you are compassionate toward us. Help us to be that way to ourselves, especially when we're weary. Thank you for understanding we are human and giving us what we need in our weakest moments. We will not quit; we will let you carry us. Amen.

· · · · ·

What are three things that help when you feel like quitting? (For example, taking a nap, spending time with an encouraging friend, going for a walk.) Write them down so you'll have them to refer to when you need them next.

GOOD GRIEF, *I am still so very human.*

—Fiercehearted

FIFTY-ONE

Whiteboard

This foolish plan of God is wiser than the wisest of human plans, and God's weakness is stronger than the greatest of human strength.

1 Corinthians 1:25 NLT

I've mentioned the whiteboard in my office. It sits in the corner like an artist's easel and I use it to figure out the universe. I do this with a mason jar full of dry erase markers in every color. I draw lines and circles, plot and plan, untangle the knots in my mind one word at a time. I like to make sense of things, you see. The only trouble is, sometimes it doesn't work. Sometimes I stand in front of that whiteboard, and when I'm finished, everything just looks like a bowl of spaghetti. I'm still confused and unsure. I walk away feeling frustrated and as if I've somehow failed.

There's nothing wrong with planning—the book of Proverbs is full of verses on the wisdom of planning. What causes trouble is when I start trusting in my plans rather than God's purposes. I know the symptoms: weariness, discouragement, stress, staring at the ceiling at night, standing in front of the whiteboard way too long. I've discovered my planning tendencies go into overdrive for one reason: fear. I'm worried that things won't work out the way I hope. I'm feeling insecure about my calling. I'm forgetting that God has brought me this far and he will not leave me now. So I think that I have to figure everything out. I need to make it all happen.

What I'm forgetting is that what God does hardly ever makes any sense at all. Making a shepherd boy the greatest king to ever rule Israel. Sending the Savior of the world to a manger. Choosing an uneducated, inexperienced group of men to spread the gospel. No one would have put that on their whiteboard. No one would have added it to a PowerPoint. No one would have thought it worthy of a bullet point in a strategic plan. *But God did.*

When I look back over my life, I see the same. I didn't know a thing about publishing when I submitted my first greeting card idea to DaySpring, the Christian subsidiary of Hallmark. But God opened the door and I worked there for a decade. My coworker and I were clueless about social media when we launched (in)courage, a website that would have almost a million page views in its first six months. I'd tried for ten years to have a baby when God unexpectedly brought a twenty-one-year-old into our lives who became the daughter we'd always wanted but never expected.

> Life isn't about our plans. It's about God's purposes.

In all those scenarios and so many more, I'm so glad the outcome wasn't dependent on what I thought should happen.

This is what I'm coming to understand: Life isn't about our plans. It's about God's purposes. He will make sure they happen even in our weakness, in our wandering, in our uncertainty.

> Many are the plans in a person's heart,
> but it is the Lord's purpose that prevails. (Prov. 19:21)

That's what makes us brave, what gives us the strength to keep going, what we can write on the whiteboard of our hearts today.

God, you are the One who knows everything—the past, present, and future. Nothing in any of those can stop your purposes from coming to pass. When we feel like it all depends on us, help us depend on you. You will do it. Amen.

• • • • •

How do you make plans—on a whiteboard, in a to-do list, with your calendar? Whatever you do, pause now and pray over your plans today before you move forward with them.

GOD IS ABSOLUTELY COMMITTED *to his plans. He is completely devoted to his promises. He is forever and ever faithful to what he's said he will do.*

—Fiercehearted

FIFTY-TWO

Powerful Weapons

Let your gentleness be evident to all. The Lord is near.

Philippians 4:5

There's one thing I've yet to learn how to plan for, that I can't seem to control: the seven billion other people who share this spinning earth with me. Perhaps you've discovered this as well.

On a recent evening, I laid my head on my pillow, soft cotton against my cheek like the palm of a mother's hand, but I couldn't be soothed. Even when I closed my eyes I could still see the fists raised, the tears shed, the blood drops on the ground.

In this noisy, broken world with the news headlines and the neighbors drawing lines and the threats on the horizon, none of us can escape this question: How am I to respond? It seems the easiest answer might be to throw the next punch, write the next rant, hold the switchblade of our opinions up to the necks of our opposers so they know we mean business.

This is our instinct, the animal inside us that is about claws and teeth and growling. It's what awoke in the apostle Peter when soldiers came to arrest Jesus in the Garden of Gethsemane. "Then Simon Peter, who had a sword, drew it and struck the high priest's servant, cutting off his right ear" (John 18:10).

It's this odd detail in a familiar story, never ever shown on any Sunday school flannel board, that keeps echoing through my mind. I finally pause and consider, *What happens when you cut off someone's ear?* I understand in a flash: the person can no longer hear you. This means so much more has been cut off too—communication, understanding, reconciliation, relationship.

I might say, "I would never cut off someone's ear!" but haven't I? My swords have been self-righteous words, criticism, judgment, dismissal of those who are different from me—folks I might even be tempted to label "the enemy." We swing the sword of our words in defense of what we believe is right, but there are unintended consequences. This is not the way of the kingdom. "Jesus commanded Peter, 'Put your sword away!'" (John 18:11).

I don't think this means we aren't to fight the darkness. But I do believe it means we are to understand there's a time and place and different way to do so. After Peter swung the sword, Jesus still got arrested. He went to trial, stretched out on a cross, rose from the grave. In doing so, he fought (and won) the greatest battle ever. Here's what stands out to me: none of this involved ear-slashing, shouting, or even sneaky finger-pointing.

Instead, Jesus fought with love. Not the fluffy, cotton-candy kind. No, the sort that is willing to be laid wide open, to sacrifice, to reach out to even our enemies. Love is still the most powerful weapon in the world.

> Love is still the most powerful weapon in the world.

He also fought with gentleness, which we so often misunderstand. It's not weakness or fear. "A gentle tongue can break a bone" (Prov. 25:15). "Always be gentle toward everyone" (Titus 3:2). Don't be fooled: *gentle is tough as nails.*

Jesus, too, chose kindness. Even on the cross he prayed, "Father, forgive them, for they do not know what they are doing" (Luke 23:34). Being kind is not the same as being "nice." Niceness is about pleasing people; kindness is about choosing to treat others as creations of God, whether or not they deserve it. "God's kindness is intended to lead you to repentance" (Rom. 2:4). *Kindness is grit in the trenches with grace.*

The clock reads midnight, the darkest part of night, the start of a new day. I whisper a prayer, "God, help me be a fiercehearted woman who lives and loves and battles like you do." I want, through Jesus, to be a heart-healer, difference-maker, and chain-breaker. "For though we live in the world, we do not wage war as the world does" (2 Cor. 10:3).

In this world, we cannot choose whether or not to be at war. *But we can choose what kind of warriors we will be.* Let's fight with love and gentleness and kindness.

In other words, let's fight like Jesus.

God, you show us what love really looks like and how it's more powerful than we can even fully understand. Love through us today in ways that change the world one heart at a time. Amen.

• • • • •

There are several verses in today's devotion. Which one speaks to you most and how can you apply it today?

A fiercehearted woman . . .

makes gentle the new strong, small the new big, ordinary the new extraordinary.

—*Fiercehearted*

FIFTY-THREE

Belt of Truth

Therefore put on the full armor of God, so that when the day of evil comes, you may be able to stand your ground, and after you have done everything, to stand. Stand firm then, with the belt of truth buckled around your waist.

Ephesians 6:13–14

We've talked about fighting for our hearts, fighting for each other, fighting like Jesus. As we near the end of our time together, I want to talk through the armor God has given us so we can do so. We'll spend the next few days exploring each piece of it together, starting with the belt of truth.

Confession: I can't remember the last time I put on a belt. One hangs in my closet, forlornly waiting to fulfill its destiny. I remember the day I bought it. How it wooed me with its cheetah print and shiny gold buckle. I thought I'd wear it with jeans, the kind that grow loose and lazy by the end of the day. Bad news for the belt: I'm in a season of preferring what's stretchy and comfortable, so I just let the jeans do their thing.

Perhaps because of this I found I didn't fully understand what Paul meant when he said about the armor of God, "Stand firm then, with the belt of truth buckled around your waist" (Eph. 6:14). I pictured the flimsy belt in my closet, but it turns out the belt described here, the kind worn by a Roman soldier, would have been eight to twelve inches tall and made of thick leather. It covered much of a soldier's torso, offering not only protection but also security and stability. It was the first piece of armor to be put on and held many of the others together.[1]

As I listened to this description by Pastor Brandon Cox, something else fluttered through my mind, a distant recollection that in ancient times the part of the body the belt covered (described as "the bowels") was seen as an important part of emotions. This is somewhat similar to how we might talk today about feeling something in our gut. If this is so, I pondered, then perhaps part of the purpose of the belt of truth is to help guard our emotions.

The other day I saw a blessing that someone in my life had and I wanted, one I had prayed for God to grant me for years. While I'm generally content with my life, in that moment the lies got loud and I felt it all—frustration, jealousy, grief. Then these words came to mind: "No good thing does [the Lord] withhold from those whose walk is blameless" (Ps. 84:11). (Note: our "walk is blameless" not because of what we do but because of what Jesus has done for us.) I whispered to my heart, "If this had been truly good for you, God would have given it. You can trust that you have his best for your life." In that moment, I felt like the arrows being shot toward me were deflected—they hit the belt of truth.

Experiencing emotions, even unwelcome ones, isn't an attack. I went to my husband later and said, "I feel sad that I don't have this in my life." He put his arms around me and let me lay my head on his shoulder until I felt better—as I imagine God does with my heart in those moments. But the *lies* I heard before those emotions came did seem like an enemy was at work. Hearing "God is holding out on you" and "You're missing out" was unbidden and entirely unhelpful. Those words were ruthlessly aimed at the most tender parts of who I am. Lies wound and destroy, truth protects and defends. That's one important way we can tell the difference between the two.

Lies wound and destroy, truth protects and defends.

My poor little belt is still waiting patiently in the closet. I imagine it sighs when it sees me put on something with an elastic waist yet again. I can't make it any promises that I'll change my behavior. But I am choosing to put on a different kind of belt these days, the belt of truth. I need its strength. I need its protection. And the really good news? This belt is available to all of us and goes with everything. Yep, even yoga pants.

God, you are the provider of everything we need for victory. Today we choose to put on the belt of truth. We will believe what you say no matter what we may hear. We will stand firm. Amen.

• • • • •

Putting on the armor of God is an intentional act. Pause and picture the belt of truth going into place around your waist now that you've prayed. What lie are you battling today? What is the truth that will defend your heart against it?

A fiercehearted woman . . .

defends like a warrior and weeps like a girl.

—Fiercehearted

FIFTY-FOUR

Breastplate of Righteousness

For in the gospel the righteousness of God is revealed—a righteousness that is by faith from first to last, just as it is written: "The righteous will live by faith."

Romans 1:17

I help facilitate a local group of writers dubbed the "Word Girls" and I recently asked them to bring a childhood photo of themselves when we got together. I wanted us all to remember what it was like to love books and writing before the pressure and professionalism.

One friend of mine pulled a photo from her purse clearly from the eighties, the sort that's slightly faded and beginning to curl up at the edges. Her hair was wispy, gathered in a ponytail, her legs and arms like the limbs of a tree in early spring.

Just as we began to tell her how cute she was, she declared, "Oh my! I'm holding up a training bra!" Sure enough, she had a flimsy bit of cotton in her hands. It dangled over a newly opened box, as if it had been presented as a gift. We all giggled because we're familiar with this rite of passage.

I begged my mama for my first bra. Never mind that I had nothing to train, protect, or promote. I wanted the symbol of it—that I was a woman somehow. Years later I most often begrudge this piece of clothing with its underwire and elastic.

It's clear the average Roman soldier would not have attended Word Girls or appreciated our laughter and laments over training bras. And this is not the kind of attire Paul had in mind when he said, "Stand firm then . . . with the breastplate of righteousness in place" (Eph. 6:14). Covering the chest for soldiers was not a matter of personal preference—it was about life and death. The breastplate (also known as body armor) protected the vital organs, especially the heart. In some instances, it was literally called a "heart guard."

What strikes me most about the breastplate is how it's described: "the breastplate *of righteousness*" (Eph. 6:14, emphasis mine). I hope you have not been under the illusion that I'm never wrong about anything, because if that's the case, then you are about to be disappointed. I have, for my whole life, made an incorrect assumption about those two words—*of righteousness*. I thought this meant that if we do what's right, then our actions help protect us. Perhaps not to the extreme that some folks do, like the ones who say, "If I'm good, then nothing bad will ever happen to me." But I still thought the righteousness I was putting on was *my* righteousness and was about what *I* did.

Here's the trouble with that thinking: Just like I had nothing to offer my poor training bra, I've got nothing to offer in terms of righteousness. "As the Scriptures say, 'No one is righteous—not even one' " (Rom. 3:10 NLT). We need someone to impart their righteousness to us. This is what happens when we place our trust in Jesus. "I no longer count on my own righteousness through obeying the law; rather, I become righteous through faith in Christ. For God's way of making us right with himself depends on faith" (Phil. 3:9 NLT).

This goes against our human nature, our desire to strive and earn and prove. Someone once said to Jesus, "We want to perform God's works, too. What should we do?" (John 6:28 NLT). I can see myself standing by for the answer, pen in hand, paper ready for me to start the long to-do list. But Jesus replied, "This is the only work God wants from you: Believe in the one he has sent" (John 6:29 NLT). Believing. Trusting. Surrendering our desire to prove we're good enough. The righteousness we receive *through Jesus alone* is our heart's hope and defense. We take what's his as ours and then he empowers us to live it out.

The righteousness we receive *through Jesus alone* is our heart's hope and defense.

My friend is not the same little girl in that picture now. She has grown up to be a warrior—someone who is tender and fierce, strong and kind, a grace-giver and fear-fighter. She has put on the breastplate of righteousness. She goes into battle with it as she prays, encourages, and serves. When I look at her heart, I see Jesus first. This is beautiful. This is powerful.

God, we acknowledge that we need your righteousness and that you have freely given it to us through Jesus. We believe you and we trust you. You are our heart's hope and defense now and forever. Amen.

· · · · ·

Putting on the armor of God is an intentional act. Pause and picture the breastplate of righteousness going into place and guarding your heart now that you've prayed. What's one area of your life where you especially need him to guard your heart today?

I SUDDENLY ASKED, "JESUS, WILL YOU BE GOOD FOR ME?" *I didn't mean "good for me" in the way we say it about broccoli or wearing sunscreen. I meant it like, "Will you be good in my place? Will you be perfect on my behalf? Will you cover over all the errors in the script of my life with the red pen that is the cross?"*

—Fiercehearted

FIFTY-FIVE

Gospel Shoes

Peace I leave with you; my peace I give you. I do not give to you as the world gives. Do not let your hearts be troubled and do not be afraid.

John 14:27

I step into the store on an ordinary Saturday morning. I'm wearing workout pants and carrying a cup of coffee. I explain to the enthusiastic sales guy who looks barely old enough to drive, has legs of solid steel, and is clearly a morning person that I need a pair of running shoes. I add that I'm using the term *running* loosely. In his world, I have a feeling it might be described more as "walking faster than normal."

He nods, undeterred, and says, "Let's get you on the treadmill!" I am unprepared for this, for any public display of my lack of athletic ability, but I cooperate. I'm videotaped from above as if I'm robbing a bank or convenience store. Then I'm shown the recording and told, "See how your feet roll in? You're unstable." Inwardly, I thought, *Well, that's not a revelation—my husband has suspected the same for years.* Outwardly, I nod and let him take me to find a pair of shoes that will cure this condition.

I learned that day what every ancient soldier knew: stability, being able to stand firm, is the most important part of footwear. But they didn't accomplish that goal through fancy tennis shoes. Instead, soldiers wore leather sandals that had something like small spikes attached to the soles. More similar to soccer cleats, these shoes allowed them to hold their ground when the enemy attacked. Paul said, "For shoes, put on the *peace* that comes from the Good News so that you will be fully prepared" (Eph. 6:15 NLT, emphasis mine).

The peace that comes from the Good News is knowing we have been made right with God and he is on our side. "The God of peace will soon crush Satan under your feet" (Rom. 16:20 NLT). We don't have to fight the attacks alone. Victory isn't up to us. We are simply told to "stand firm" (Eph. 6:14). God will do it. He will deliver us. He will bring us through the battle. The peace we have *with* God means we can have peace *within* us regardless of what happens around us.

MacLaren's Commentary says about Ephesians 6:15: "The quiet heart will be able to fling its whole strength into its work. And that is what troubled hearts never can do, for half their energy is taken up in steadying or quieting themselves, or is dissipated in going after a hundred other things. But when we are wholly engaged in quiet fellowship with Jesus Christ we have the whole of our energies at our command, and can fling ourselves wholly into our work for him."[1] And what is our work? We've talked about this before: It's to "believe in the one he has sent" (John 6:29 NLT). We fight by faith.

The most powerful warrior is the one who can hold on to peace even in the middle of the battle.

The most powerful warrior is the one who can hold on to peace even in the middle of the battle. This is what Jesus offers us. "I have told you these things, so that in me you may have peace. In this world you will have trouble. But take heart! I have overcome the world" (John 16:33). Oh, our knees may knock and our hands may tremble. There will be tears and sweat and hard days. That's okay. Peace is not simply an emotion. Instead, peace is a position we take of standing on who God is, what he has promised, and who he tells us we are no matter what happens.

Let's put on our shoes today. Let's stand firm together.

God, you are our peace. You are the One who brings victory in our lives. You make us stand firm. We choose to plant our feet on who you are, on your Word, on what you've promised today. Amen.

• • • • •

Putting on the armor of God is an intentional act. Pause and picture the shoes of peace going into place and empowering you to stand firm today. Think of a time when you experienced peace in the middle of a difficulty. What did God show you through that time?

We become sneaky ninjas

in tennis shoes and fuzzy slippers. We who are all softness and grace on the outside are tough as steel on the inside.

—Fiercehearted

FIFTY-SIX

Shield of Faith

Faith is confidence in what we hope for and assurance about what we do not see.

Hebrews 11:1

A friend of mine showed me her book cover this morning. It's not yet published and seeing it felt a bit like looking at an ultrasound photo of a baby in the womb. I was struck by the wonder that this book would soon be birthed into the world. At the top of the cover there's an arrow that looks as if it's flying toward an unknown target on the other side of the page. It's a symbol of freedom and strength, beauty and boldness.

But there are uglier arrows in our world. "Take up the shield of faith, with which you can extinguish all the flaming arrows of the evil one," Paul said in Ephesians 6:16. These arrows are not benign. Not for show. No, the sort of arrows Paul would have been familiar with were weapons of destruction. They were tipped with a combustible material and then lit on fire. To guard themselves against such attacks, soldiers had a shield so large that it covered most of their body when they were standing on a battlefield.

When I read "Take up the shield of faith," I can tend to think, *The bigness or boldness of my belief is what matters*. But this changes when I consider that David the psalmist described God over and over as his shield. "God is . . . my shield, the power that saves me, and my place of safety" (Ps. 18:2 NLT). It's not the size or strength of our faith that matters. It's Who we're placing it in that makes all the difference.

> It's not the size or strength of our faith that matters. It's Who we're placing it in that makes all the difference.

When I looked closer at the elements of ancient shields, I almost fell out of my chair because while soldiers likely never realized it, I see God so present throughout each layer.

First, the shield itself was made out of wood. When we take up the shield of faith, we are placing ourselves behind the protection and redemption of the cross—who Jesus is and what he has done on our behalf.

Then the wood was covered by leather, by animal skins—a reminder of sacrifice. God gave his only Son on our behalf, and this sacrifice saves us.

The leather of the shield was frequently rubbed down with oil or soaked in water, which was the invisible secret to extinguishing flaming arrows. This sounds a lot like anointing and baptism, both of which are related to the Holy Spirit. It is the truth imparted to us by the Spirit that quenches the fiery arrows the enemy shoots at us—the lies, accusations, and temptations.

With all this in mind, it becomes clear that taking up the shield of faith means simply placing our trust in who God is and what he has done for us. And we never need to be afraid that our belief feels small or weak. That's exactly why we need the shield of faith—because we are human and we falter. But even "if we are faithless, he remains faithful" (2 Tim. 2:13). It's not about our faith but God's faithfulness. "His faithfulness will be your shield" (Ps. 91:4).

The enemy would like to convince us that if we struggle with doubt, if we have days when we don't "feel" what's true, if we wrestle with questions or have moments when nothing makes sense, then all is lost. The fight is over.

But that isn't true. When an ancient soldier was under the most intense attack, the best position to be in was *on his knees.* That's when the shield was most effective because it covered the entire soldier.

This is the battle-winning secret: when we don't have the strength or will or wisdom to fight, we don't have to; we only need to be still and let God cover us.

God, you are our shield. What you did for us on the cross, your sacrifice on our behalf, the power of your Spirit is where we place our trust. When we are weak, you are strong. When we are faithless, you are faithful. Cover us in every way today. Amen.

· · · · ·

Putting on the armor of God is an intentional act. Pause and picture yourself picking up the shield of faith. What's an area of life where you feel under attack? Tell God and ask him to cover you today.

FOR SO MANY YEARS I DIDN'T KNOW—*I really didn't—that someone could be used by God, especially in a very public way, and still be fighting battles every day.*

—Fiercehearted

FIFTY-SEVEN

Wear Your Helmet

Don't worry about anything; instead, pray about everything. Tell God what you need, and thank him for all he has done. Then you will experience God's peace, which exceeds anything we can understand. His peace will guard your hearts and minds as you live in Christ Jesus.

Philippians 4:6–7 NLT

I have a particular skill. It's one I've possessed since childhood. I've nurtured and raised it like a prize-winning Rottweiler. I, quite simply, am a champion worrier. I inherited at least some of this skill from my sweet mama, whose girlhood nickname was "Worry Wart." She got it from a long list of nervous relatives in our lineage.

The truth is, I want better than worry for my mama and all my Jesus sisters and my own heart too. Instead of worry, I want peace for us. I want rest. I want settledness and contentment. But as with many things we've put up with for a long time, worry is hard to let go of. That's why I was intrigued when I read that we are to "take up the helmet of salvation." It seems this piece of equipment is quite clearly designed to protect our minds, which is where worry tries to take hold.

This phrase, the helmet of salvation, is used in two other places in Scripture. God himself is the first to wear it. Way back in the Old Testament, "He . . . placed the helmet of salvation on his head" (Isa. 59:17 NLT). What this tells me is that the helmet we put on is not our own. Salvation isn't something we earn or invent. Instead, it's something always and only given to us by God.

In the second mention, Paul tells us to live, "wearing as our helmet the confidence of our salvation" (1 Thess. 5:8 NLT). Yes, this confidence in our salvation is about eternal hope, but the armor of God passage is clearly about the here and now, about the battlefield we find ourselves on today. So what does it actually look like to "take up" and "wear" the helmet we've been given? It seems Philippians 4:6 gives us a list:

> Don't worry about anything.
>
> Instead, pray about everything.
>
> Tell God what you need.
>
> Thank him for all he has done.

The result of all these actions is what makes me feel they're related to the helmet of salvation: "Then you will experience God's peace, which exceeds anything we can understand. His peace will *guard your hearts and minds* as you live in Christ Jesus" (Phil. 4:7 NLT, emphasis mine). This is the helmet of salvation at work. When we're confident in God's love for us, we can come to him in the middle of the battle, in the hardest places. We can tell him what concerns us and trust he will take care of us. We can live in gratitude because we know he is faithful. Then his peace will guard our minds—even in the midst of all-out war.

I called worry a talent, but really it's a troublemaker. It's a joy-stealer and fear-bringer and day-ruiner. I need a defense against it. I'm so glad God offers me one. But it's up to me to take it up and wear it. I do this when I focus on

God instead of my current circumstances or future scenarios that evoke fear in me. Worship weakens worry.

The helmet of salvation surely has many other applications, many other ways it benefits us. But this defense against worry is the one I need most right now, right here, in this very moment. Maybe the same is true of you too.

We are not worriers; we are warriors.

If so, we don't have to let worry win today. Oh, this doesn't mean it will be easy. We're talking about a battle, after all. About fighting hard. About sometimes getting knocked down. God understands this, but he also knows the identity and destiny he's given us. We are not worriers; we are warriors.

God, you are the One who gives us salvation. We can't ever earn it; we can only receive it through your grace. Then from that place of confidence we can come to you with whatever we need and you will guard our hearts and minds. We choose worship over worry today. Amen.

· · · · ·

Putting on the armor of God is an intentional act. Pause and picture placing the helmet of salvation on your head, covering your mind today. What is one of your worries? Share it with God and then replace it with worship.

I have let worry run off

with my joy like a thief in the night over and over again. Lock the door and bar the windows of your heart to worry this second, honey. The real danger is not what you imagine might happen but the thief himself. You're really so much more secure than you feel.

—Fiercehearted

FIFTY-EIGHT

Sword of the Spirit

The word of God is alive and active. Sharper than any double-edged sword.

Hebrews 4:12

My parents have a home movie of my brother and me that can only be shown on a film projector. I haven't seen it for years (because who has a film projector these days?), but I remember the scene. I'm about four, my brother close to two. I've got blonde hair. He has brown curls. We each have a pillow shoved right up our shirts and we're bouncing, giddily, on a bed. Occasionally, we lock arms and one of us throws the other down. I have no clue where we got this idea, but we have decided on this day we are sumo wrestlers.

I can treat encounters with the enemy of my heart as if it's much the same, as if it's just casual and silly, all fun and games until someone gets hurt. That someone is usually me. Maybe I often don't see it coming because pillow sumo wrestling is basically my only combat experience. But as I am now a grown-up, it seems time I became better prepared for the skirmishes I do face as a believer.

In the armor of God, there's only one piece that's actually used not just for defense but for fighting back. "Take . . . the sword of the Spirit, which is the word of God" (Eph. 6:17). This is not the kind of shiny silver sword carried by princes in cartoon movies. Pastor and author Brandon Cox said the kind of weapon mentioned in this passage is actually more like a small dagger to be used in hand-to-hand combat. He also said that *word* in this verse doesn't mean big, broad truth. Instead, in the ancient language, it's *rhema*, which more accurately describes a particular truth for a particular situation.[1]

This description makes me think of Jesus during the temptation. The exchange between him and the devil reads like a hand-to-hand combat scene where words are the weapons.

> The devil said to him, "If you are the Son of God, tell this stone to become bread."
> Jesus answered, "It is written: 'Man shall not live on bread alone.'" . . .
> He said to him . . . "If you worship me, it will all be yours."
> Jesus answered, "It is written: 'Worship the Lord your God and serve him only.'" . . .
> "If you are the Son of God," he said, "throw yourself down from here." . . .
> Jesus answered, "It is said: 'Do not put the Lord your God to the test.'"
>
> (Luke 4:3–4, 6–9, 12)

Jesus won this showdown by knowing and declaring specific spiritual truth. For us to be prepared for what we may face from the enemy, it's essential that we spend time in God's Word. I've heard this kind of statement from folks who have used it to induce guilt, who have said that I must do so in a particular time, way, or amount. This is not what I'm saying to us today. God's Word is intended to be a weapon of love and freedom, never of shame, guilt, or fear.

God's Word is intended to be a weapon of love and freedom, never of shame, guilt, or fear.

It's okay to find a way of connecting with God's Word that fits with who he has made you. If you're a morning person, reading the Bible as soon as you wake up might be natural and easy. But you might be an auditory learner who needs to listen to Scripture as an audiobook in the car. You may be a verbal processor who benefits most from going through verses out loud with someone else. The point isn't how we engage with God's Word, it's simply that we do.

Thankfully, there were no swords involved in my bed-jumping, sumo-wrestling childhood days. But I'm a woman now, with a real enemy. I also have a real God who equips me (and you) with everything we need to win. His help and strength are ours for the taking.

We only need to say the word.

God, you are the living Word, the One who gives us the truth we need for victory. Give us ears that hear and hearts that remember what you say so we will be mighty in battle, prepared for whatever we may face. Amen.

· · · · ·

Putting on the armor of God is an intentional act. Pause and picture picking up the sword of the Spirit, which is the word of God, and carrying it with you today. What is one of your favorite Scripture verses? Write it below as a reminder of the truth and power it holds.

I REMEMBER OPENING THAT BIBLE *one day and reading a few lines. I told God then and there I wanted Jesus to be my Savior and for him to have my whole heart, for my whole life.*

—Fiercehearted

FIFTY-NINE

As We Are

Thanks be to God! He gives us the victory through our Lord Jesus Christ.

1 Corinthians 15:57

Yesterday morning I sat across from a friend in a coffee shop. The sun slanted through the windows and bounced off the surface of the table between us. She ordered a cinnamon roll the size of my face. She let me have part of it. Because this is what friends do.

We'd both just come through weeks of turmoil and a few tears. We felt battle worn and a bit weary. But we also felt strong and brave and true. "Years ago, we wouldn't have done this," we said to each other. "We would have hidden. We would have backed down. We would have let fear win."

But not now. Not anymore.

A few minutes ago I talked with another friend who is still right in the middle of the surge. She is afraid and she wants to quit, but she keeps saying, "I have to see this through because it's about more than just me." I know she will.

When I think of all three of our situations, and so many more I see in my real life and online, I realize we are a generation of warriors. We may not ever be recognized as such. Because we fight not with anger but with grace. We defend not with force but with kindness. And we know this secret—God himself *is* love and nothing is impossible with him.

This doesn't mean we need to have it all together. It doesn't require a spotless life. We are not supposed to have all the answers. I think it simply means we speak the truth of our stories, the truth of the God we love, where we are right now and as best as we know how.

We're fiercehearted women who are here for such a time as this.

At the beginning of our time together I invited you to sit in the coffee shop with me too. And if we were face-to-face now, I'd say to you, "We're fiercehearted women who are here for such a time as this." We are in nurseries and boardrooms. We are in homes and high-rises. We are in schools and senior retirement centers. A fiercehearted force to be reckoned with. We are strong, brave, and loved.

God, in you we have everything we need for whatever we may face. As long as we are in this world, we will face hard things, but we can take heart because you are the great Overcomer. It is well with our souls. Amen.

. . . . .

When has God brought victory in a circumstance or situation in your life? Thank him for that again as a reminder that he will do the same for whatever you're facing today.

"We learned to live fully and love bravely."

It's not a poem or a declaration. It's not a manifesto or a creed. Not a doctrine or a proclamation. It's just what I still believe deep down we all can do. It's the story of the fiercehearted.

—*Fiercehearted*

SIXTY

Embrace Your Story

Being confident of this, that he who began a good work in you will carry it on to completion until the day of Christ Jesus.

Philippians 1:6

We started our sixty days together talking about stories, about a friend of mine who shared hers on a black stool that swivels. And we are coming full circle, because we, fiercehearted women, are all living a story today. A story crafted and told by the Author of heaven. The star-scatterer. The mountain-mover. The water-walker. It is a story of being brave and strong and loved. A story of, most of all, love.

In the day-to-day, it doesn't feel like a story. It feels like dishes in the sink. Reports on the desk. Another mile behind the steering wheel of the car. But this doesn't change what's real. Beneath the surface of all that ordinary still shines the glory.

Sometimes the plot is confusing. Or strange. Or sad. Sometimes we want to cut out a chapter with sharp scissors. Sometimes we want to be the editors with the red ink. Sometimes we want to skip right to the end just to make sure it says, "And they lived happily ever after."

But this is not our role. It is not for us to say, "This is what happens next" or "I'm changing the ending." Instead, we are to trust, to wait, to be in the middle of the mystery. There is so much we do not know, that we will not know, but we can be certain of this: the Author is good and we are loved.

Yes, even when the unexpected sentence comes. When we face that dark-as-night period. When the syllables jumble together and we scratch our heads. Even in those places, between those lines, there is a God at work who has always been speaking, always been creating beauty out of the broken. "Jesus also did many other things. If they were all written down, I suppose the whole world could not contain the books that would be written" (John 21:25 NLT).

Jesus is *still* doing many other things. He is not done with history. He is not finished with the part of it that is our story either. Whatever scene we find ourselves in today, it is not the final page. Hold on, there is a turning coming. There is more than this, more than here and now. We have not yet seen the there and then.

Whatever the future brings, our God is still holding the pen. He is the only one who gets to write, "The End."

We are overcomers. We are warriors. We are a force to be reckoned with in this world. And whatever the future brings, our God is still holding the pen. He is the only one who gets to write, "The End."

God, you are the Author of our lives. You are writing a powerful story of grace in and through us. Help us be fiercehearted women for you every day, on every page of our lives. We love you. Amen.

· · · · ·

Think back over the last sixty entries. What's one truth God has spoken to your heart that you will take with you into whatever is next in your story?

MAYBE REAL COURAGE *is simply bearing witness to the wild and mysterious story God has always been writing. Perhaps true success is finally believing our actual, everyday part in his story is good . . . and good enough.*

—Fiercehearted

More Resources

Thank you so much for going on this *Strong, Brave, Loved* journey!

If you'd like more encouragement, you can find it in *Fiercehearted: Live Fully, Love Bravely* and Holley's other books, such as *You're Already Amazing*. If you'd like content to do with a group, check out the *You're Already Amazing LifeGrowth Guide*.

You can also stop by holleygerth.com for more content, tools, and resources. While you're there, you can sign up for devotional messages to be sent right to your inbox. And you can find Holley on Facebook, Instagram, Twitter, and Pinterest.

Holley is passionate about empowering girls in poverty to grow up to be fiercehearted women. You can find out more at compassion.com/fiercehearted.

Cheering you on, fiercehearted woman!

Acknowledgments

Writing *Fiercehearted* and now *Strong, Brave, Loved* has reminded me again that life is a journey and those who walk with us make all the difference.

Thank you to my wonderful team at Revell—Jennifer Leep, Wendy Wetzel, and Amy Ballor. You are not only fantastic partners but also dear friends. I'm so grateful for the years we've spent together, and I look forward to what's ahead!

To my virtual assistant, Kaitlyn Bouchillon—your diligence, excellence, creativity, and friendship matter more than you could ever know. I appreciate all you do.

To my parents, Don and Lyn Armstrong—I'm so thankful for all the wonderful memories I have because of you. You love me so well and pray for me so faithfully. So much of who I have become is because of you.

To my grandmother, Eula Armstrong—I'm so blessed by the legacy of faith you have given me. You are an example of resilience and following Jesus for a lifetime. I'm so proud of you.

To my daughter, Lovelle—you are a gift from God to your dad and me. We are grateful every day that he brought us together. You are a remarkable woman and were worth every minute of the wait.

Acknowledgments

To my husband, Mark—there are hardly enough words to describe all you are to me. Partner, friend, encourager, and the man I will be in love with all my life. I'm thankful every day to share this adventure with you.

To my dear friends who were cheerleaders, advisors, and prayer warriors while I wrote *Fiercehearted*, especially the Word Girls, Kim Sawatzky, Kristen Strong, Jennifer Watson, Ellen Graf-Martin, Kara Bird, Jennifer Dukes Lee, and Renee Swope. You bring so much joy to my life and add so much goodness to my words. Let's have coffee soon.

Most of all, to Jesus—thank you for the privilege of being part of the work you're doing in this generation. I pray that all I write will bring you glory and delight. Everything we do and all we are is about and for you. Amen.

Notes

Chapter 1 Dangerous Women

1. Priscilla Shirer, “A Woman’s Battle Plan for Victory,” Fervent Tour (Cross Church, Springdale, AR, February 15, 2016).

Chapter 4 Gut Honest

1. See http://bravegirlcommunity.com/bravegirl-christy/; http://gracehillschurch.com/women/.

Chapter 12 Love over Fear

1. Suzanne Eller, “Overcoming Fear of the Future” (video), Facebook, November 8, 2016, https://www.facebook.com/SuzanneEllerP31/videos/10154460461815266/.

Chapter 35 Barefaced Beauty

1. Brené Brown, *The Gifts of Imperfection: Let Go of Who You Think You’re Supposed to Be and Embrace Who You Are* (Center City, MN: Hazelden, 2010), chap. 2, Kindle.

Chapter 36 Gentle

1. Mark Schatzman, “Gentleness” (sermon), August 12, 2017, Fellowship Bible Church, MP3 audio, https://www.fellowshipnwa.org/listen-feed/2931.

Chapter 37 Parade

1. President Theodore Roosevelt, “Citizenship in a Republic” (speech), the Sorbonne, Paris, France, April 23, 1910, http://www.theodore-roosevelt.com/trsorbonnespeech.html.

Chapter 42 Rest, Trust, Repeat

1. Jess Connolly and Hayley Morgan, *Wild and Free: A Hope-Filled Anthem for the Woman Who Feels She Is Both Too Much and Never Enough* (Grand Rapids: Zondervan, 2016), chap. 2, Kindle.

Chapter 49 Awkward

1. *Nashville*, season 4, episode 17, "Baby Come Home," directed by Jet Wilkinson, aired April 27, 2016.

Chapter 53 Belt of Truth

1. Brandon Cox, "Getting Dressed for Battle" (video), Facebook, April 15, 2018, https://www.facebook.com/gracehillsnwa/videos/1654419854640969/.

Chapter 55 Gospel Shoes

1. Alexander MacLaren, "Ephesians: A Soldier's Shoes," in *MacLaren's Commentary* (*Expositions of Holy Scripture*), BibleHub, accessed February 12, 2019, http://biblehub.com/commentaries/ephesians/6-15.htm.

Chapter 58 Sword of the Spirit

1. Cox, "Getting Dressed for Battle."

About Holley

(THE OFFICIAL STUFF)

HOLLEY GERTH wishes she could have coffee with you. And if she could, she'd never mention any of this, because she'd be too busy listening to you and loving it.

Holley is the *Wall Street Journal* bestselling author of *You're Already Amazing* as well as several other books. She's also a licensed counselor, certified life coach, and speaker who provides encouragement as well as practical insights for the thousands of people she connects with each year.

Holley cofounded (in)courage.me, an online destination for women that received almost one million page views in its first six months. And her personal site, holleygerth.com, serves over thirty thousand subscribers.

Outside the word world, Holley is the wife of Mark, and together they're parents to Lovelle—a daughter they adopted when she was twenty-one years old because God is full of surprises. Holley would love for you to hang out with her at www.holleygerth.com.

CONNECT WITH

Holley

HOLLEYGERTH.COM

@HolleyGerth